CONTENTS

INTRODUCTION

BY JUDD APATOW

Knocked Up was the first film I have made that was written with the assistance of BlackBerry technology. I have been using a BlackBerry since the year 2000, when we were shooting our college-themed television show *Undeclared*. One day I realized that I was spending a lot of time on set, and that maybe there was some way to get some writing done between setups. Then it struck me—I could outline future episodes on my BlackBerry and then e-mail them to myself.

So that is exactly what I did. As I waited around for sets to be lit or actors to arrive, I would send long e-mails to myself with fragments of outlines, and sometimes even fully completed outlines. What was even stranger was that when I read the e-mails, there was a lot of good stuff in there. Those ideas were not garbage!

Flash forward to the year 2005. Now I am a completely addicted BlackBerry user. You know the kind—the ones who put the BlackBerry on their night tables and stare at them all night long to see if the light indicating a new message has illuminated. The kind who types into it while having a conversation with you, and only hears 8 percent of what you say while nodding. The kind you want to punch in the face—hard.

I had just completed *The 40-Year-Old Virgin* and was very busy running around trying to make sure the publicity and marketing were in good enough shape so that it might succeed and I could hopefully get the chance to make another film. But at the same time I had an idea for a new film, and the ideas were coming fast. So I started using the BlackBerry to e-mail myself the ideas that would one day become *Knocked Up*. In the subject line I would write "pregnancy" so they would one day be easy to locate among my voluminous list of e-mails.

I thought it might be amusing to show you some of those e-mails. Actually, I am not sure how amusing it is, but it is the only idea I have for this introduction.

Here is one of the first e-mails.

From: Judd Apatow
Date: August 7, 2005 12:57 PM
To: Judd Apatow
Subject: Pregnancy

A couple gets pregnant on the first date.

Older sister of the woman has kids and represents its difficulties and complications.

Going through this helps her adjust her life in a positive way. She doesn't like Seth. Maybe Seth admits she is right at some point.

Seth's parents are willing to let them live with them. But that is the last thing the girl wants to do.

We can show them meet. The first encounter. How it leads to sex. Not using birth control can be a major point of contention for the whole film. Why didn't they use it? The idea of being forced into a relationship for life is the main conflict. A relationship in reverse. A baby, then get to know one another. A friend can say, "No matter what, you guys are stuck dealing with each other till you die." Also the sister can fill her younger sister with all the questions that the sister can't believe she doesn't know the answers to yet. Which leads to the couple fighting. The rush to get to know each other quickly. For the girl there can be a sense that this is the end of her dreams, vocationally. Her ability to finish school etc. is impossible unless they become a team. There could be an exploration of adoption. Maybe even private adoption. Seth could have a friend who was adopted and is crazy and is violently against it. A friend of hers can be very pro abortion. That is explored. Documentaries watched. Should they find out if it is a boy or girl is a big debate and fight.

Religion. Maybe she keeps thinking he'll run till finally she forces him to run. The idea of the film is that their idea for their lives is altered completely. Freedom is gone. Tracks are laid down permanently and it causes break-downs. What about my year living in Europe or etc. So the end is realizing this is a bizarre gift and that the woman is as well. But she should not be the kind of person he thought he would wind up with. She could work with her sister. Running a shop of some type. Something he knows nothing about and cares nothing about. He can't even fake it. Like clothes. We see them attempt interest in each other's work. They have to meet friends, which couldn't be more awkward. They could have huge fights about her drinking. He thinks she is pushing it. She says you are allowed to drink a glass of wine. She is a little more reckless than he is comfortable with. And then he can't get it up because he doesn't want to hurt the baby. He could design menus for dvd's or something with computers. Need a non hacky work environment. He could spend a lot of time on computer.

What if at some point Leslie gets pregnant. Or thought she was.

Leslie says spend a day with me and see what it's like, then it is hellish in every way. Seth spends time with Rudd in some way. They lie about what they are gonna do, then get drunk in a bar.

There are so many things you can't say.

Maybe Rudd complains like crazy about family life and then is always sweet with kids, and Seth realizes he is all talk. And just blowing off steam.

Seth is panicked to get career and money going in the middle.

She wants sex to start labor. "I'm fat." "I don't want to crush and poke the baby." She is past her due date.

How do we move time forward? Smoking. She has trouble quitting. Weight. Has issues with gaining weight, stretch marks, the first time she sees them she hates him. The movie should be about the fact that he falls in love with her first, but she takes longer and isn't sure. She is terrified, doesn't trust him. At some point she goes off on him so hard that he runs and she completely flips out. Suicidal even. And what happens is he proves his devotion. He commits to the idea of committing forever and she eventually sees this, feels safe and falls hard for him.

She feels like she is letting everyone down. Him meeting her mom is a big sequence. He gets so nervous that when he is introduced to her brother, he leans in to kiss him like he is a woman, then stops at the last moment. The baby forces everyone to face the reality of their situations. We can move time by having a montage of him at doctor's appts. Looking uncomfortable. With doctor's hands in her. Happy montage. Broken-up sequence. Almost fistfight with other pregnant woman. Bed rest. Suddenly huge boobs which squirt milk, or she wants him to get them going for the baby. Mucous plug. Baby class. But not married. Hospital tour.

A shocking amount of that made it into the movie. I guess I never warmed to the crazy-adopted-friend idea. I still like the idea of Alison getting pregnant, then having a real hard time quitting smoking. But the movie was two hours and nine minutes long, with credits, so I don't think there is a huge cry out there for me to have made the movie longer.

Here is how the birthday party and bouncer sequence looked in the original e-mail.

From: Judd Apatow
Date: September 21, 2005 8:39 AM
To: Judd Apatow
Subject: Pregnancy

At birthday party Rudd and Leslie get back together quickly. Seth is stuck. Maybe tries and fails.

Leslie goes off on the bouncer at the club. The guy breaks and apologizes. "I am sorry. It is because you're old. They don't want old people, 'cause then we become old club. I am also not allowed to let in more than five percent blacks and Asians, and one percent middle eastern. It is fucked. I have been so guilty about it but I need the job."

Then cut to Leslie crying on a corner.

People often ask about our use of improvisation. You can tell from the original idea of this scene that it is a clean setup for people who are hilarious, like Craig and Leslie, to riff on that rejection. Once the feelings are clear, it becomes much easier for us to play on set.

Here are some other e-mails that might amuse.

```
From: Judd Apatow
Date: September 6, 2005 8:20 AM
To: Judd Apatow
Subject: Pregnancy
```

Rudd is a liar. Says he has meetings. Goes to coffee shop
or the movies. During a fight Seth tells Leslie.

Seth never told Leslie, but the other part was the main idea of Paul Rudd's storyline. I personally have never told my wife that I had an appointment and went to the movies instead, but I can't say I haven't fantasized about it. It is strange how these thoughts come to you. Sometimes they come quick, from out of nowhere. Slowly I have come to the realization that they come to me for a reason and that I should take them very seriously.

```
From: Judd Apatow
Date: September 6, 2005 8:23 AM
To: Judd Apatow
Subject: Pregnancy
```

Rudd has tricks for babies and marriage, like leaning the
baby out when he holds it so it does not feel safe and
reaches for Mom. Then he can watch TV.

Start movie with guys in Vegas having so much fun. She
interviews star for E! or morning news. Gets promotion to
on camera.

Later during break, up they go to Vegas and it sucks.

She doesn't tell bosses she is pregnant. Thinks they are
not allowed to fire her.

At dinner Rudd and Leslie fight over who takes the baby outside when it cries.

"But I just got my appetizer."

"But I was with them all day."

Rudd explains to Seth about giving in. It's like Judo. You
really win.

At end of the film you find out Leslie is pregnant and they
have been trying for years. Seth is mad at Rudd for it.

Seth gets job writing video games.

They fight about their job. "Oh, you think interviewing
Pierce Brosnan is gonna change the world."

One other idea I had that I did not use was a sequence where Ben gets
Debbie, Alison, and Pete stoned at Debbie's house. Suddenly one of the
kids starts crying, and Pete and Debbie get into a fight about who should
soothe the child. Both feel guilty for smoking pot for the first time in ages,
and they get paranoid and freak out, thinking the child will know, or that they
will not be able to safely deal with the child.

Another idea that didn't make it in was based on something Katherine
Heigl improvised one night. She went on a great run about how she is
seven months' pregnant and her maternal instinct hasn't kicked in. It was a
great area, but it came up too late in shooting to be fully explored. I love
the idea of a woman in total panic because she does not feel emotionally con-
nected to the unborn baby. It is the kind of feeling that many people get.
"What if I never start caring enough to be a great parent?"

From: Judd Apatow
Date: February 4, 2006 10:38 AM
To: Judd Apatow
Subject: Pregnancy

Rudd: I read that there are tons of pharmaceuticals in the
drinking water.

Leslie: What did it say? Specifically?

I don't remember. I only read the headline.

So you are just gonna put that out there and make me paranoid and give me no details whatsoever? What paper was it
in?

I don't remember, it was the Internet.

Can't you check your Internet history?

That stuff erases automatically. It was a few weeks ago.

I hate the way you communicate.

This was basically taken verbatim from a discussion Leslie and I had one morning. She was so irritated that I read something that meant harm to our family and didn't bother to remember any detail about it. I guess other men would be out buying water filters or looking for homes near clear water. I have no excuse. I was lame.

From: Judd Apatow
Date: May 19, 2006 7:58 AM
To: Judd Apatow
Subject: Pregnancy

Sadie: "When you are not around he makes the biggest blowers."

"What are blowers?"

"Farts. They sound like a walrus with a bone stuck in his nose and a cold."

Sadie likes him.

"Ben's here. I like him. He's funny."

Leslie: "So? Where does that get you?"

"Funny people are nice."

Also at party.

Seth: "How come you get forgiven and I don't?"

"We're married. She has no choice but to forgive me. What else is she gonna do?"

I had written, and we shot, a bunch of moments where Alison and Debbie debate the merits of Ben being funny. Alison takes it to mean he is a good guy. In one take Debbie responds, "Who cares? What do you want to marry Bob Hope? Fuck funny."

From: Judd Apatow
March 5, 2006 6:49 PM

```
To: Judd Apatow
Subject: Pregnancy
```

Leslie's role should be brave. It should be tough, and
sweet, and nasty and break your heart.

To Rudd: "Why wouldn't you want to be here?"

Rudd needs an answer.

"Sometimes you judge me so much and push so much, I want to
run away. I can't be perfect. I can't heal your wound. I am
here, but you will never believe I am gonna stay. And I am.
But sometimes I need to go to a hockey game."

Pause. Does she get it?

"Get out."

Need a reason why the nightclub relates to this. Does she
need to know she is young and doesn't need him?

Do we need to understand that Alison doesn't want to be
like Debbie, scared, insecure? So she goes the other way
and dumps Ben.

The subtext of the nightclub scene is that Debbie is unhappy in her marriage, and somewhere in her mind she is thinking, "If I am gonna leave this guy, I better do it while I am still young so I can meet a good man." That is why it is so brutal when the bouncer won't let her in. It is not about the club, it is about getting stuck with her detached husband.

My intention with this storyline was to have the audience think Debbie is a ballbuster in the first half of the film and side with Pete. He is cute and funny, so she must be the problem. But then, as they reveal themselves, you realize that Pete is emotionally shut down, insecure, and flippant when it comes to his family life, and that Debbie has been driven almost mad by this behavior. Then at the end you see them together, continuing to work on their marriage, which I think is a very noble thing to do. But that is probably because my parents got divorced when I was a kid and I want no couples to get divorced, ever.

```
From: Judd Apatow
April 2, 2006 4:32 PM
```

To: Judd Apatow
Subject: Pregnancy

Shoot improvs with Seth and Maude.

If I shoot the kids from across the room so it is mainly
someone's pov of them, it will be easier to get usable
material.

Maude can speak the truth.

She calls him Fred Flintstone. "Cause you look like him."

At the party she says, "They said bad things about you, but
I stood up for you. They said you loved your bong more than
my aunt. What's a bong?"

"Do you like Barney?"

"I'm eight. I like Gwen Stefani."

Looking at this now I think I should have used the bong joke, not what
I eventually used, which was Sadie saying "Blah-blah-blah. Ben's a prick." My
daughter Maude, who played Sadie, does not remember saying that word, but
when she is eventually able to see the film, when she is eighteen, I wish it
was "bong" she'd hear. I'm sorry, Maude.

From: Judd Apatow
April 13, 2006 9:18 AM
To: Judd Apatow
Subject: Pregnancy

Rudd: Do you live here?

Seth: She refuses to sleep at my place till we clean our
bathroom, and my roommates won't do it.

This is another area I did not explore enough—Alison forced to hang out
with Ben's friends. We shot some funny moments where she hangs out with
each friend, just for safety, but I should have found a way to build it into the
story. It would have been very funny. On our DVD is a deleted scene of Alison

and Jonah watching *Brokeback Mountain,* which is funny, but also really offensive. I apologize to everyone associated with that film, also.

Anyway, that is a brief look inside my head as I write. I hope you enjoyed it. I would like to thank my wife, Leslie Mann, for collaborating with me, inspiring me, and tolerating me, as well as all the actors whose vital contributions made this film possible. Enjoy reading the script. Writing it was a very enjoyable, fulfilling experience for me. It was the first time I found the courage to be deeply personal in my work. I hope I find that courage again one day.

—Judd Apatow

Maude and Iris Apatow

KNOCKED UP

by

Judd Apatow

EXT. BEN'S HOUSE - DAY

BEN STONE, 23, cute in a chunky Jewish guy sort of way, boxes one of his roommates, MARTIN. His other roommates, JAY and JASON fight with broom sticks. JONAH drinks beer on the couch spectating.

Quick Images:

* We see Ben and Jay fighting. At one point they fight with gloves which are on fire, balancing on a plank over a dirty pool.

* Ben now has a fishbowl filled with weed smoke over his head. There is a smoking joint in his mouth, making the bowl get cloudier and cloudier. He starts coughing hysterically and takes it off.

*A boom box is playing. The boys are now free style rapping. It is terrible but they are having a blast. Pot is being smoked. Beer is around.

EXT. AMUSEMENT PARK - A DIFFERENT DAY

Ben and roommates ride a terrifying rollercoaster.

INT. ALISON'S BEDROOM - MORNING

ALISON SCOTT, pretty, 24, wakes up to her radio alarm.

INT. DEBBIE AND PETE'S HOUSE, BEDROOM

Alison's sister, DEBBIE, sleeps on the floor of the bedroom, while her husband, PETE, sleeps on the bed with their eight-year-old daughter SADIE. CHARLOTTE, age three, jumps on the bed.

                    CHARLOTTE
          Sadie, wake up.

                    SADIE
          Oh my gosh.

                    CHARLOTTE
          Daddy, wake up.

Charlotte hits Pete.

                    PETE
          Okay, I'm up.

EXT. BACKYARD - MORNING

She exits a guest house and walks to the main house dressed for work.

INT. KITCHEN - MORNING

Debbie, is making breakfast for Charlotte and Sadie. Pete enters the kitchen.

                    DEBBIE
          I need you to take the kids to school
          this morning.

                    PETE
          Oh, I would, but I'm supposed to work
          out.

                    DEBBIE
          What?

                    PETE
          I got an appointment with a trainer. I
          can't cancel now, he'll charge me.

                    DEBBIE
          Well, you didn't tell me.

                    PETE
          Yeah I did. Last week, I told you.

                    DEBBIE
          You didn't tell me.

                    PETE
          I did. And then I wrote it on the
          calendar like you told me to.

                    DEBBIE
          No, you didn't tell me.

                    PETE
          I did tell you.

                    DEBBIE
          Well, you didn't, but what are we going
          to do? Because I have an appointment so
          you're taking the kids to school.

Pete holds Charlotte in front of him.

                    DEBBIE (cont'd)
          Don't use the baby to cover your tracks.

                    ALISON
          I can drive them. I'll drive them to
          school.

                    PETE
          Thank you very much.

                    DEBBIE
          Great. Good. You turned my sister into a
          limo driver.

                    ALISON
          I don't mind.

                    PETE
                 (to Charlotte)
          It all worked out!

INT. ALISON'S CAR - DAY

Alison drives the kids to school. Charlotte and Sadie sit in
the back. Charlotte GIGGLES.

                    ALISON
          What are you giggling about?

                    SADIE
              (to Charlotte)
     Be quiet. You're starting to annoy me.

                    CHARLOTTE
     Poo poo.

                    ALISON
     Ladies. Nice.

                    SADIE
     You know what I did the other day?

                    ALISON
     What?

                    SADIE
     I Googled "murder."

                    ALISON
     You Googled "murder?"

                    SADIE
     Yeah.

                    ALISON
     Why? I mean what did it say?

                    SADIE
     It didn't say anything. It just showed
     pictures of people lying dead on the
     floor and...blood everywhere and ugh...

                    ALISON
     That was just ketchup.
              (beat)
     Who wants to hear some music?

                    SADIE
     I want to hear "Rent."

                    CHARLOTTE
     I want to hear Green Day!

                    SADIE
     No, we're listening to "Rent."

                    CHARLOTTE
     Well, I want to listen to Green Day.

Sadies takes Charlotte's doll.

                    SADIE
     Well, I got your baby!

Charlotte WHINES.

                    ALISON
     Don't taunt her. Come on.

                    SADIE
     Here.

Sadie shoves the doll at Charlotte.

                    ALISON
Sadie!

                    CHARLOTTE
    (crying)
Ow!

                    ALISON
Why did you just do that? Don't throw
things at your sister!

                    CHARLOTTE
She hit me.

                    ALISON
Did you hit her?

                    SADIE
I did not.

                    ALISON
Make her happy.

    (to Charlotte)
It's okay.

                    SADIE
It won't make her happy. She spilled all
the marbles on the floor.

                    ALISON
Well, give her her marbles back.

INT. BEN'S HOUSE - DAY

In a living room of the house the guys have created an office
for their web site. There are a few large tables, several
computers which they work at, and a few TV sets which have
movies running on them. Ben and his friends are holding a
meeting. They each have a note pad and pen, and Jonah is on a
computer. They smoke a joint and drink beers.

                    JASON
All right? Now, are you sure you
understand the terms of the bet? 'Cause
this is serious.

                    MARTIN
Oh, no.

                    JASON
Martin, listen. You don't shave your
beard or cut your hair for one year, and
if you can do that, I will pay your rent.
But if you shave, then you have to pay
all five of our rents.

                    MARTIN
Thanks for the free money, bitch.

                    JONAH
Hey, Martin, was it weird when you joined
the Taliban, being American and
everything like that? Like when you see a
woman driving a car, do you just get
pissed?

                    JASON
Just watch your back, Serpico. You never
know who your friends are.

                    MARTIN
You guys can't make fun of me the whole
time.

                    JASON
But, Martin, it's a competition. It's
called "The Dirty Man Competition." We're
gonna make fun of you until you shave the
beard. That's the rules.

                    JAY
That's the whole point. You're supposed
to be tempted into shaving.

                    BEN
Your face looks like Robin Williams'
knuckles.

                    MARTIN
You guys aren't allowed to make fun of
me. It's not part of the rules.

                    JASON
Martin, why didn't you just listen to me
when I was explaining the rules? You just
looked at me with that blank stare of
yours. It was like talking to a wax
statue.

                    BEN
Okay, guys, are you ready? So... "Only at
'Flesh of the Stars.com' will customers
be able to find exactly how long into
what movies their favorite stars are
exposed."

                    JASON
Nice.

                    JAY
Oh, fuckin' booya.

                    BEN
Pretty good, right?

                    JONAH
Yeah.

                    JASON
Yeah, ka-ching. Ka-ching. Ka-ching.

                    JONAH
Guys, let's start loggin', all right?
Charles Manson? Do you have any other
thoughts?

                    MARTIN
Good, awesome, let's start this off with
a bang. Jamie Lee Curtis. I got an hour
and ten minutes in "Trading Places." Uh,
both chesticles.

                    JAY
          Ah, I got something. A three-titted alien
          from "Total Recall?"

                    JONAH
          Aw, she's not famous.

                    JASON
               (imitating Schwarzenegger)
          "Damn it, Cohaagen, give the people the
          air."

INT. E ENTERTAINMENT TELEVISION STUDIO - DAY

RYAN SEACREST stands in front of a series of cameras. Alison
stands behind with a clipboard and headset.

                    RYAN SEACREST
          So if you want that perfect tan like the
          stars, he's the one to see. We'll be
          right back on "E! News." Stay with us.

                    ALISON
               (into her headset)
          Okay.

                    RYAN SEACREST
          Okay, is Jessica Simpson here yet?

                    ALISON
          Let me check.

                    RYAN SEACREST
          Is she on her way?

                    ALISON
          Hey, guys?

                    RYAN SEACREST
          She's left her house?

                    ALISON
               (into her headset)
          Okay, let me know when she's pulling in.

               (to Ryan)
          She's about to pull in.

                    RYAN SEACREST
          Is she camera-ready?

                    ALISON
               (into her headset)
          Is she camera-ready?

                    RYAN SEACREST
          If she's going to be in hair and makeup
          for three hours. I can't do it. I'm not
          going to be here. I got to do "American
          Idol." It's live. I got to do it. I got
          to be there. What are we going to
          interview her about?

                    ALISON
          Nothing personal.

                    RYAN SEACREST
No personal questions.

                    ALISON
No personal questions. Don't ask her
about her sister and her nose job.

                    RYAN SEACREST
No plastic surgery questions.

                    ALISON
She doesn't want to talk about her boobs
or her father's comments about her boobs.

                    RYAN SEACREST
Great. We'll talk about the Middle East
and maybe an idea of an exit strategy.
Maybe she has a good pitch. Should I ask
her about Korea? Maybe have her point it
out to us on a globe? I don't understand
the young talent in this town! It doesn't
make any sense. I got four jobs. Hell,
I'm more famous than half the people we
talk to anyway! No one stands up. No one
has the balls to sit them down and say,
"Look, just cut the shit."But everybody
works for 'em. They're all on the
payroll. They're all sucking the teat!
Nobody sits 'em down, eye-to-eye, one-on-
one, and says... "Cut the shit." And all
these stars just to fuck it up. That's
what they do. They fuck my day up! And it
pisses me off! And now I'm sweating.

                    ALISON
You know what? You want us to just come
and get you when she gets here? You want
to head to the green room for a minute?
Just chill out?

                    RYAN SEACREST
That's a good idea.

                    ALISON
Want us to bring you anything? You want
some water?

                    RYAN SEACREST
No.

                    ALISON
You want a cookie?

                    RYAN SEACREST
Cookie, yeah, cookie. Thanks.

                    ALISON
Okay, we'll get you a cookie.

                    RYAN SEACREST
I'm sorry I'm pissy.

JILL, one of the E! executives, approaches Alison.

                    JILL
Alison?

                    ALISON
Yeah?

                    JILL
Jack and I need to see you in his office.

INT. JACK'S OFFICE, E! ENTERTAINMENT - DAY

Alison's boss, JACK, early forties, is at his desk. Alison
and Jill sit in the office.

                    JACK
Thanks for coming in, Alison. Well, we
wanted to talk to you today because we
had a little debate on the conference
call with New York about you.

                    ALISON
You were talking about me?

                    JACK
We were wondering aloud to one another
whether or not you would be good for on-
camera.

                    ALISON
What'd you decide?

                    JILL
They decided that they like you. And they
would like to put you on camera.

                    ALISON
Really?

                    JILL
I know. I was so surprised, too.

                    ALISON
Oh, my God. This is the best news ever.
Thank you so much. This is great!

                    JACK
Congratulations.

                    ALISON
Thank you.

                    JACK
I'll take that smile as a "Yes, I'll do
it."

                    ALISON
Absolutely. I'm so excited. Oh, my God.

                    JILL
It's a lot of work. Can't wait to see
what happens. It's going to be tough.
Tough job.

                    JACK
About the work, most immediately, there's
going to be some things that you're going
to be able to get that other people in
the office don't get. One of them: Gym
membership.

                    ALISON
You want me to lose weight?

                    JACK
I don't want you to lose weight.

                    JILL
We can't legally ask you to do that.

                    JACK
We didn't say lose weight.

                    JILL
No.

                    JACK
I might say "tighten."

                    ALISON
"Tight."

                    JACK
A little...tighter?

                    JILL
Just like toned and smaller.

                    JACK
Don't make everything smaller. I don't
want to generalize that way. Tighter.

                    JILL
We don't want you to lose weight. We just
want you to be healthy.

                    ALISON
Okay.

                    JILL
You know, by, by eating less. We would
just like it if you...go home and step on
the scale and write down how much you
weigh and subtract it by, like, twenty.

                    ALISON
Twenty.

                    JILL
And then weigh that much.

                    JACK
Just remember, you've got it here, you've
got it here, and everybody's going see
you right there.

INT. HOUSE - NIGHT

Debbie and Alison hug. Pete is on the couch wearing
headphones.

                    DEBBIE
Yay! That's so exciting!

                    ALISON
Yay!

                         DEBBIE
          Oh my god!

               (to Pete)
          Hey!

                         PETE
          Huh?

                         ALISON
          I got a promotion.

                         PETE
          Oh, congratulations!

                         ALISON
          Thank you.

                         PETE
          Hey, maybe you can get your own place
          now.

                         ALISON
          Oh, let's not get ahead of ourselves.
          Yay!

                         DEBBIE
          Let's go celebrate.

                         ALISON
          Okay, let's do it.

                         DEBBIE
          Pete'll watch the kids?

                         PETE
          Yeah! We can watch "Taxicab Confessions."

                         DEBBIE
          What are you going to do?

                         ALISON
          I don't know!

Debbie and Alison SHRIEK.

                         DEBBIE
          I'm so excited.

                         ALISON
          Yay!

INT. CAR - NIGHT

Alison and Debbie drive to a nightclub.

                         DEBBIE
          I walked in on him masturbating one
          night.

                         ALISON
          Ooh! Did you get the deer-in-the-
          headlights look? Did he freeze or did he
          finish?

> DEBBIE
> No, he tried to pretend like he wasn't
> doing anything under the covers.

> ALISON
> Oh, no!

> DEBBIE
> I buy these nice towels and he whacks off
> into them.

> ALISON
> "Deb and Pete forever"

> DEBBIE
> And once he does that into them once,
> they're never soft ever again.

EXT. NIGHTCLUB - NIGHT

Alison and Debbie are walking over.

> DEBBIE
> I can always tell if I'm looking good
> based on whether or not we get in.

They reach the front. The Bouncer looks at them and waves
them in.

> BOUNCER
> Ladies?

> ALISON
> Guess we're looking good.

> DEBBIE
> If I didn't get in, I would have lost my
> shit.

Ben and the guys are standing at the head of the line.

> BEN
> What's going on man? How long you gonna
> make us wait out here, for Christ's sake?

> JAY
> Come on! What the fuck!

INT. NIGHTCLUB

Ben sits with his friends, Jason, Jonah, Jay, and Martin.

> BEN
> You know what movie I just saw again the
> other day which is fucking, like, mind-
> blowing, and I haven't seen it since it
> came out? "Munich."

> JAY
> "Munich!"

> JONAH
> Dude, "Munich" fuckin' rules.

> JAY
> "Munich" is awesome!

                    BEN
          That movie was Eric Bana kicking fuckin'
          ass!

They all agree.

                    BEN (cont'd)
          Dude, every movie with Jews, we're the
          ones getting killed. "Munich" flips it on
          its ear. We cappin' motherfuckers.

                    JONAH
          Not only killing, but fuckin', like,
          takin' names.

                    BEN
          If any of us get laid tonight, it's
          because of Eric Bana in "Munich."

                    JONAH
          I agree with that.

                    JAY
          I agree.

                    BEN
          You know what is not helping us get laid?
          Is the shoe bomber, Richard Reid, over
          here at our table. I like your shoes.

                    JONAH
          How was "Burning Man" this year?

                    MARTIN
          Fuck you guys, I'm glad I'm not Jewish.

                    BEN
          So are we.

                    MARTIN
          Fine. Screw it.

                    BEN
          You weren't "chosen" for a reason.

                    JAY
          Yeah. Ahh!

                    JASON
          Ohh!!!

Meanwhile, Debbie and Alison head for the bar.

                    DEBBIE
          It's like everyone in here is twelve
          years old.

Debbie SIGHS.

                    DEBBIE (cont'd)
          Am I too old to be here?

                    ALISON
          What?

                    DEBBIE
          Am I too old to be here?

                    ALISON
          No, of course not.

                    DEBBIE
          Does it look weird that I'm here?

                    ALISON
          No, not at all.

                    DEBBIE
          Am I hotter than these little bitches?

                    ALISON
          Yes! You look amazing.

                    DEBBIE
          Guys in here would fuck me, right?

                    ALISON
          Yes.

                    DEBBIE
          That's weird to say, but, it makes me
          feel better.

                    ALISON
          You look hot.

                    DEBBIE
          I believe you.

                    ALISON
          I'm getting us drinks.

Alison leaves for the bar.

INT. NIGHTCLUB BAR - MOMENTS LATER

Ben is already at the bar attempting to get the BARTENDER's
attention.

                    BEN
          Yo, a beer over here, please? You're
          gonna be embarrassed when you realize I'm
          Wilmer Valderrama. God.

                    ALISON
               (to the Bartender)
          Oh, Hey! Excuse me!

                    BEN
          He's literally ignoring this entire half
          of the bar. Don't even bother.

                    ALISON
          Yeah, awesome.

                    BEN
          A beer over here, please? He looked at
          us! Did you see that?

                    ALISON
          Yeah, that was rough.

                    BEN
          And if *you* can't get service, what am I
          gonna do, you know?

                    ALISON
          Great. It's going to be that night.

                    BEN
          Okay, you want a beer?

                    ALISON
          Yeah.

                    BEN
          Just observe.

Ben leans over the bar and picks up two bottles of beer and
drops money on the bar.

                    BEN (cont'd)
          There you go.

                    BARTENDER
          Come on, man!

                    BEN
          Here you go! For your trouble! Thank you.

Ben hands one beer to Alison

                    BEN (cont'd)
               (to Alison)
          There you go.

                    ALISON
          Thank you.

                    BEN
          Okay, enjoy it.

                    ALISON
          Are you sure?

                    BEN
          I'm sure. I tried that once before at The
          Comedy Store and I got punched in the
          ear.

                    ALISON
          Thanks a lot, Oh, fuck, fuck! I'm
          supposed to get one for my sister.

                    BEN
          Oh, here, take mine.

Ben hands Alison his beer.

                    ALISON
          No, that's okay. I'll wait. I'll, he'll
          get me--

                    BEN
               (interrupting)
          Please, I very rarely look cool. This is
          a big moment for me. Just take it.

                    ALISON
        Thank you. Awesome.

                    BEN
        No problem.

                    ALISON
        I'm Alison.

                    BEN
        I'm Ben.

An awkward beat passes between them.

                    ALISON
        Well, have a great night.

                    BEN
        Okay, you too. Have a--

                    ALISON
        Thanks for the beer.

                    BEN
        Okay, enjoy, be nice to them.

                    ALISON
        Bye. Thanks again.

Alison leaves the bar to rejoin Debbie.

                    BEN
        I'll see ya later.
            (to himself)
        No, I won't, 'cause I'm a pussy.

INT. NIGHTCLUB - CONTINUOUS

Ben rejoins his friends.

                    JASON
        What's up, daddy?

                    BEN
        That girl. She, she totally gave me an
        opening, man, and I locked up. I just
        want to get shit-faced, though, you know?
        I'll just jerk it later. It's cool.

                    JASON
        Are you fuckin' crazy, man? She
        looks...smart. Who's that she's sitting
        with?

                    BEN
        It's her sister.

                    JASON
        Her sister?

                    BEN
        Yeah.

                    JASON
        Dude, it's the dream. What are we doin'
        standing here man? Let's go.
            (MORE)

                    JASON (cont'd)
Come on, follow me.

          (to Martin)
You stay here.

                    MARTIN
Why?

                    JASON
'Cause your face looks like a vagina.

                    MARTIN
Dick!

Ben and Jason head toward Alison and Debbie.

                    JASON
Hey, which one's the sister?

Jonah approaches Martin.

                    JONAH
Hey, Crockett. You still partyin' with
Tubbs these days?

                    MARTIN
Come on, man. I'm getting it from all
angles here. I don't like it anymore.

                    JONAH
I know, I don't either. Was it weird when
you changed your name from Cat Stevens to
Yusuf Islam?

                    MARTIN
Yeah, it was really awkward.

                    JONAH
All right, man. I got to take off. See
ya, "Scorsese on coke."

Jay GROWLS loudly.

                    MARTIN
What's that?

                    JAY
Chewbacca. It's, you know, it's Chewie.

                    MARTIN
Oh, another beard joke.

                    JAY
Fuck.

                    MARTIN
Fuckin' hilarious!

Meanwhile, Ben and Jason get to Alison and Debbie's table.

                    BEN
Hey.

                    ALISON
Hey.

                    BEN
Hi, this is my friend, Jason. I just
wanted to see how my beers were doin'.

                    ALISON
This is my sister, Debbie.

                    BEN
Oh, hi, I'm Ben.

                    DEBBIE
Hi, Ben?

                    BEN
Yes.

                    DEBBIE
Nice to meet you.

                    JASON
How ya doin'?

                    DEBBIE
Good, how are you?

                    JASON
Just trying not to stare.

                    ALISON
She's married.

                    DEBBIE
        (to Alison)
Why do you have to say that?

                    ALISON
What?

                    JASON
It's a shame. You're beautiful.

                    DEBBIE
Thank you.

                    ALISON
She has two kids, too.

                    DEBBIE
Shut up!

                    ALISON
What? It's nothing to be ashamed of.

                    BEN
You think that's gonna stop him from
hitting on her? It's not, at all.

                    JASON
I love kids.

                    DEBBIE
Really?

                    JASON
Yeah, absolutely.

Debbie's cell phone RINGS.

                    DEBBIE
          Excuse me.
               (into the phone)
          Hello?

                    BEN
          Cool phone.

                    ALISON
          Yeah, she's got a really cool phone.

                    DEBBIE
               (into the phone)
          What? Is it a rash or is it the chicken
          pox? I don't know! Google it. Okay. All
          right, bye.
               (to Alison et al)
          I got to go. Sadie might have the chicken
          pox.

                    JASON
          I had the chicken pox three times. I have
          no immunity to it.

                    BEN
          We don't have the heart to tell him it's
          herpes.

                    JASON
          It's not herpes if it's everywhere.

                    DEBBIE
               (to Alison)
          Are you coming?

Alison and Ben exchange a strange look.

                    ALISON
          Um, uh, you know, I'm all dressed, so
          I'll just hang out.

                    DEBBIE
          Really?

                    ALISON
          Yeah, I'll take a cab home.

                    DEBBIE
          Be safe.

                    ALISON
          I will.

                    JASON
          Bye, lovely.

                    DEBBIE
          Bye.

Debbie leaves.

                         JASON
          All right, I'm gonna let you two get to
          know each other.

INT. NIGHTCLUB - NIGHT

QUICK CUTS

*Ben and Alison talking, dancing and drinking.

                         BEN
          Cheers.

                         ALISON
          Cheers.

                         BEN
          To you.

*Ben and Alison take pictures of each other with their cell
phones.

                         ALISON
          No, no. You know, the like, Entertainment
          News channel?

                         BEN
          Oh, E!

                         ALISON
          E!

*Ben and Alison dance, clearly pretty drunk now. We see
Ben's friends in the background, also dancing. Ben pretends
to throw dice while dancing.

                         JONAH
          Dude, I think he's doing the dice thing
          too much.

                         JAY
          That's really all he's got.

*Alison and Ben take another shot. Alison runs her fingers
through Ben's hair.

                         ALISON
          I love your curly hair! It's so great. Do
          you, like, use product or anything? You
          put anything in it?

                         BEN
          I use Jew. You want to get out of here?

                         ALISON
          Yeah, let's go. We can go hang out at my
          place?

                         BEN
          Yes, uh, uh, uh...

                         ALISON
          I'll show you my audition tape.

                         BEN
          Wicked.

                         ALISON
          It's really funny.

                         BEN
          Okay, I'm really excited to watch that.

They exit the club.

EXT. NIGHTCLUB - MOMENTS LATER

Alison and Ben stagger out of the club and head down the
sidewalk.

                         BEN
          We should get a cab.

Ben grabs Alison and they kiss.

EXT. BACKYARD - LATER

Ben and Alison stagger across Pete and Debbie's yard towards
the guest house.

                         BEN
          This is a big yard!

                         ALISON
          Shh!

                         BEN
          Let's go swimming right now. Let's just
          do that.

                         ALISON
          No.

                         BEN
          I'm doin'-- Whoo!

INT. ALISON'S BEDROOM - MOMENTS LATER

Alison and Ben collapse on the bed and make out. They take
off their shirts.

                         BEN
          You're prettier than I am.

They continue to make out.

                         ALISON
          Do you have a condom?

                         BEN
          I do.

                         ALISON
          Okay.

                         BEN
          It's in my pants. I have a condom.

                         ALISON
          Okay.

                         BEN
          I'll get it.

Ben grabs his pants and takes out a condom.

                         BEN (cont'd)
          Man.

Ben struggles to put on the condom.

                         BEN (cont'd)
          Come on.

                         ALISON
          Hurry up.

                         BEN
               (to the condom)
          Stupid fucker.

                         ALISON
          What are you doing?

                         BEN
          I almost got it. Just give me a second.

                         ALISON
          Oh, God, just do it already!

                         BEN
          Okay.

Ben throws the condom on the floor and rolls over onto
Alison.

                         BEN (cont'd)
          Good thing I'm drunk. This is lasting
          forever.

                         ALISON
          Yeah, it's awesome.

                         BEN
          I just doubled my record time.
               (beat)
          I'm sorry I'm sweating on you.

                         ALISON
          Okay, just stop taking.

EXT. GUEST HOUSE - MORNING

Establishing shot of the guest house in morning light.

INT. GUEST HOUSE - MORNING

Ben is SNORING, his ass fully exposed. Alison is wide awake,
clearly kept up by his unattractive snoring. She stares at
him, not sure how she feels about what happened last night.

She nudges him with her foot.

                         BEN
          Fuck off, Martin. I said, fuck off
          Martin.

Ben awakens and turns around.

                         ALISON
          Hi.

                         BEN
          Oh. Hey.

                         ALISON
          Hey.

Ben assesses the situation.

                         BEN
          I'm naked.

                         ALISON
          Yeah.

                         BEN
               (whispering)
          Did we have sex?

                         ALISON
          Yes.

                         BEN
          Nice.
               (beat)
          What time is it?

                         ALISON
          Seven-thirty.

                         BEN
          Why the fuck are we awake? Let's go back
          to sleep.

                         ALISON
          I have to go to work.

                         BEN
          Really?

                         ALISON
          Do you need to get to work or anything?

                         BEN
          No work today. Do you want to get
          breakfast?

                         ALISON
          Okay.

EXT. GUEST HOUSE - MORNING

Alison and Ben walk to their cars. Suddenly Pete walks out
of the house with the kids.

                         ALISON
          'Morning.

                    PETE
          Good morning Alison.

                    BEN
          I'm Ben. What's happenin', man?

                    PETE
          Ben.

                    BEN
          How's it goin'?

Pete shakes Ben's hand and smiles.

                    PETE
                 (playfully)
          Ah, to be young.

                    ALISON
          Stop it.

                    PETE
          You stop it.

                    ALISON
          See ya later.

                    BEN
          All righty.

                    PETE
          See ya later. Enjoy the day.
                 (to Charlotte)
          Never do what they did.

                    CHARLOTTE
          I'm gonna do it.

                    PETE
          You are? Uh-oh. Someone's getting home-
          schooled.

INT. DINER - DAY

Alison is in the booth. Ben emerges from the bathroom.

                    BEN
          Whew. I just yacked, something nasty. I
          feel way better, though. I think that's
          the secret. You just gotta puke. Did you
          puke?

                    ALISON
          No.

                    BEN
          You can. I won't think it's gross or
          anything.

                    ALISON
          I'm fine.

                    BEN
          Oh, okay.

              ALISON
I just need some coffee, so...

              BEN
You know, the best thing for a hangover's
weed. Do you smoke? Do you smoke weed?

              ALISON
Not really.

              BEN
You don't?

              ALISON
No.

              BEN
At all?

              ALISON
Mm-mm.

              BEN
Like in the morning?

              ALISON
No, I just don't.

              BEN
It's the best medicine. 'Cause it fixes
everything. Jonah broke his elbow once.
We just got high and, it still clicks,
but, I mean, he's okay.

              ALISON
Right.

              BEN
Yeah. Last night was great...what I
remember of it?

              ALISON
Right, yeah.

              BEN
Yeah.

              ALISON
We had a great time.

              BEN
Yeah. So what do you do?

              ALISON
I work at E!

              BEN
The television channel?

              ALISON
Uh-huh, remember?

              BEN
Wow.

                    ALISON
We had, we had this conversation last
night. I, I told you about my promotion
and I was out celebrating it. No?

                    BEN
I don't remember that at all.

                    ALISON
I'm super excited about it. I'm actually
doing my first on-air interview today.

                    BEN
With who?

                    ALISON
Matthew Fox.

                    BEN
Matthew Fox from "Lost?"

                    ALISON
Yeah.

                    BEN
You know what's interesting about him?

                    ALISON
What?

                    BEN
Nothing. Will you tell him he's an
asshole for me?

                    ALISON
No.

                    BEN
Someone needs to. Like who gives a shit?

                    ALISON
I hope a lot of people actually because
that's what my job entails, is making
sure people care about what he has to
say. I'm interviewing him.

                    BEN
Maybe it's just me. Maybe I just don't
give a shit. I'm just saying he deserves
a beat down.

                    ALISON
It's sort of embarrassing to ask at this
point, but what do you do for work?

                    BEN
Me and my roommates have started...we're
starting an Internet website.

                    ALISON
Oh, cool, what is it?

                    BEN
I'll give you the virtual experience
okay? How's that? You're at your
computer. Who's an actress you like?

                    ALISON
Mary Tyler Moore?

                    BEN
No, that does not work at all. Let's say
you love Meg Ryan.

                    ALISON
I do.

                    BEN
Great. Who doesn't? Let's say you like
her so much, you want to know every movie
where she shows her tits. And not just
that, but how long into that movie she
shows her tits. Come to our web page,
exclusively, type in 'Meg Ryan.' Bam! 'In
the Cut,' thirty-eight minutes in, forty-
eight minutes in, like an hour and ten
minutes in. She's like naked that whole
fuckin' movie. She does full-frontal in
that movie.

                    ALISON
         (disgusted)
Wow.

                    BEN
They should have called her Harry, not
Sally.

                    ALISON
Really.

                    BEN
I'll show it to you. I'll show you Meg
Ryan's bush.

                    ALISON
         (exasperated)
Okay.

                    BEN
Cool.

                    ALISON
I actually need to get going, so.

                    BEN
Awesome. Can I get your number?

Alison is incredulous.

                    BEN (cont'd)
We had fun, right? We should hook up
again.

                    ALISON
I'm gonna give you my card because
that'll be the best way...

                    BEN
If you want to contact me, I don't have a
cell right now because of payment
complications, but you can email me at
the web page, I check it. It's Ben at
flesh of the stars, one word, dot com.

Alison gets out of the booth. Ben gets up too.

                    BEN (cont'd)
          So, awesome.

                    ALISON
          All right then. Nice to meet you.

Ben puts his arms out for a hug. Alison complies. Ben kisses
the air.

                    ALISON (cont'd)
          Take care.

                    BEN
          Okay, uh, see ya.

Alison exits the diner.

                    BEN (cont'd)
          Bye!
               (to himself)
          That was fuckin' brutal. Yeah, that was
          brutal.

CARD: 8 WEEKS LATER

INT. E ENTERTAINMENT TELEVISION STUDIO - DAY

Alison is standing on stage with JAMES FRANCO.

                    ALISON
          Hi, I'm Alison Scott and we're here today
          with James Franco from "Spider Man."

                    ALISON (cont'd)
          How are you?

                    JAMES FRANCO
          Great.

                    ALISON
          Thanks for coming.

                    JAMES FRANCO
          Of course.

                    ALISON
          Tell me, were you a big fan...

Alison GULPS and appears uncomfortable.

                    ALISON (cont'd)
          ...I'm sorry, let me take that again.

                    JAMES FRANCO
          Okay.

                    ALISON
          Tell me, were you a big fan of the comic
          books growing up?

                    JAMES FRANCO
          No, actually, I didn't read any of the
          comic books until I got the movie.

Alison stares at the floor looking ill. She breathes heavily.

                    JAMES FRANCO (cont'd)
          Are you okay?

                    ALISON
          Uh-huh. Yeah, just, what about the comic
          books? Keep talking.

                    JAMES FRANCO
          Like I said I really wasn't into them,
          but now that I did the research, I think
          they're pretty amazing.

Alison runs offstage and VOMITS into a trash can. Repeatedly.

                    JAMES FRANCO (cont'd)
          What the fuck?

Alison continues to puke.

INT. EDITING BAY

Alison and her editor, BRENT, are watching the Franco/puking
clips.

                    BRENT
          Is that the sound of you puking?

                    JAMES FRANCO (ON TV MONITOR)
          If this is one of those fuckin' joke
          shows, I'm not into it.

                    BRENT
          We should put this on YouTube.

                    ALISON
          Shut up.

                    BRENT
          This is hilarious.

                    ALISON
          You're an asshole.

                    BRENT
          Look how sweaty you are. You look like
          Dom DeLuise.

                    ALISON
          I don't need to see it again. It's gonna
          make me throw up.

                    BRENT
          You look like Jabba the Hutt dying.

Brent HISSES like Jabba the Hutt.

                    ALISON
          You're such an asshole.

                    BRENT
          I'm just jerking your chain. I'll fix
          this. No problem.

                    ALISON
          Yeah, maybe if you can just edit this out
          and we can re--

Alison swallows hard.

                    ALISON (cont'd)
          --we can reshoot my questions.

Alison looks ill again.

                    BRENT
          What's up?

Alison is frantically looking for a place to vomit.

                    BRENT ('cont'd)
          Whoa, whoa, whoa, no, no, no. Over here.
          Not on the mixing board, not on the
          mixing board.

Alison finds the trash and VOMITS.

                    BRENT (cont'd)
          Are you okay?

                    ALISON
          Oh my god. Oh my god.

                    BRENT
          Are you sick?

                    ALISON
          I don't know.

                    BRENT
          What'd you eat?

                    ALISON
          I haven't eaten today yet.

                    BRENT
          You haven't eaten yet?

                    ALISON
          Do you have a napkin or something?

Brent grabs a stray piece of paper.

                    BRENT
          Here, here. What do you have, like the
          flu?

                    ALISON
          I don't know.

                    BRENT
          God, I hope you're not pregnant.

                    ALISON
          It's impossible. You have to have sex to
          get pregnant.

Alison reacts with a sad realization. Brent picks up the
phone.

> BRENT
> (into the phone)
> B.K. It's Brent Master Five. Alison just
> puked. Dude, that's what I said. She's
> probably pregnant, right?

> ALISON
> Oh, shit.

> BRENT
> (into the phone)
> How does she look right now? She looks
> like she just realized that she's
> pregnant.

INT. DEBBIE AND PETE'S HOUSE, BEDROOM - NIGHT

Debbie and Alison are sitting on the bed.

> ALISON
> No, I can't be pregnant. Right? That was
> what, eight weeks ago?

> DEBBIE
> Did you miss your period?

> ALISON
> No. Wait. I don't know. Shit. I don't
> know. I can't remember. I was, I mean,
> I've been really stressed at work. I
> can't remember my last period.

> DEBBIE
> Are you the lady who doesn't realize
> she's pregnant until she's sitting on the
> toilet and a kid pops out?

> ALISON
> Can you not joke right now? Don't joke
> right now. This is really serious.

> DEBBIE
> Did I meet him?

> ALISON
> Yeah. You know, he was kind of like
> medium height, sort of...chubby. Blonde,
> curly hair. Remember?

> DEBBIE
> With the man boobs.

> ALISON
> Yes! Here, I have this thing of him on my
> phone.

Alison takes out her phone to play a video.

> BEN (ON PHONE VIDEO)
> Hey! I live in your phone! This is the
> best night of my life! I gotta pee.

> DEBBIE
> Oh god. How did this happen?

> ALISON
> Oh, shit.

                         DEBBIE
          Well there's only one way to find out.

INT. DRUG STORE

Alison and Debbie run down the aisles looking for pregnancy
tests.

                         DEBBIE
          They're here! Here they are! Over here!

Every test on the shelf is pulled into their basket.

                         ALISON
          Okay. "Positive Choice."

                         DEBBIE
          "Easy, One, Two, Three."

They run toward the check out counter.

INT. DEBBIE AND PETE'S HOUSE, BATHROOM - MOMENTS LATER

They dump all the tests on the floor. Alison sits on the
toilet and rips one test open. She puts the applicator
between her legs.

                         ALISON
          Here. Hurry up now. Come on.

The test reads positive.

                         ALISON (cont'd)
          Get more! Get me a few more!

                         DEBBIE
          Did you try the "Ova-Sure?"

Alison furiously drinks some juice.

                         ALISON
          I'm dripping, I'm dripping. Wait.

They check another test.

                         DEBBIE
          Good! A smiley face! Oh, I think that's
          bad.

                         ALISON
          How long does this one take?

                         DEBBIE
          These can't all be positive. Let me try
          one.

Pete enters to see Debbie sitting on the toilet. Debbie
urinates on the test and checks it.

                         ALISON
          God, you really had to pee.

Debbie picks up a test. It's positive.

                    DEBBIE
          What is this? What the hell is this?

                    ALISON
          I think you picked up the wrong one.

                    DEBBIE
          Fuck. That scared me. That would suck.

Alison glares at Debbie.

                    DEBBIE (cont'd)
          I'm sorry. That scared me.

EXT. DEBBIE AND PETE'S HOUSE, POOL - NIGHT

Alison is on a chaise lounge. Debbie is sitting nearby.

                    ALISON
          It's gonna be fine. Right?

Debbie contemplates.

                    ALISON (cont'd)
          Right?

                    DEBBIE
          Of course it will be fine. It's gonna be
          fine.

                    ALISON
          Shit.

                    DEBBIE
          You just need to call him.

                    ALISON
          Maybe I don't need to call him until
          after I see the doctor.

                    DEBBIE
          You need to call.

                    ALISON
          I don't want to call him. I don't need to
          call him.

                    DEBBIE
          You should call.

                    ALISON
          I can't call him anyway. He doesn't even
          have a phone. He didn't even have a
          number to give me.

                    DEBBIE
          He doesn't have a phone?

                    ALISON
          Said some kind of billing issue.

                    DEBBIE
          He can't afford a phone? Sadie has a
          phone.

                    ALISON
          Shit, you're right. I got to call. I
          don't know. I'm gonna have to look him up
          on his stupid website.

                    DEBBIE
          What kind of website does he have?

INT. DEBBIE AND PETE'S HOUSE, OFFICE

Debbie and Alison sit at the computer looking at Flesh Of the
Stars.

                    DEBBIE
          He spelling "coming" wrong. Oh it's
          "cum." That's gross.

                    ALISON
          Just go to "Contact Us."

                    DEBBIE
          Ben?

                    ALISON
          Yeah.

Debbie begins to type the email.

                    DEBBIE
          "What is your number? I need to speak
          with you right away." Send?

                    ALISON
          Yep.

                    DEBBIE
          You're sure?

                    ALISON
          Yeah.

EXT. BEN'S HOUSE - NIGHT

Ben and his roommates are sitting around smoking weed.

                    JAY
          I love weed.

                    JONAH
          I could smoke weed every second of every
          day.

Ben wears a gas mask attached to a bong.

                    BEN
               (through the mask)
          Jay, I am your stoner.

Everyony LAUGHS.

Jason sits with his laptop.

                    JASON
          Hey, Benjamin?

                    BEN
          Yeah.

                    JASON
          "Flesh of the Stars" just got an e-mail.

                    BEN
          Really?

                    JASON
          Would you like me to read it to you?

                    BEN
          Yeah, sure.

                    JASON
          "Ben, what is your number? I need to
          speak to you right away. Alison Scott"

                    BEN, JASON & JONAH
          Ohhhhhh!

                    BEN
          Shit! Someone wants seconds, mama!

Jason types a reply while Ben watches on.

                    JASON
          "Looking forward to speaking with you."

                    BEN
          Yeah. Do one of those smiley faces at the
          end. Fuckin' A. Those are sexy.

                    JASON
          Sent.

INT. DEBBIE AND PETE'S HOUSE, OFFICE

Alison paces as she dials Ben's number.

EXT. BEN'S HOUSE

The phone RINGS.

                    BEN
          Uh-oh!

                    JAY
          Somebody wants another piece!

                    BEN
          Shhh....

                    JAY
              (whispering)
          Booty, booty, booty call.

INTERCUT:

                    BEN
              (into the phone)
          Hello?

              ALISON
         (into the phone)
   Hi, Ben, this is Alison. I don't know if
   you remember me.

              BEN
         (into the phone)
   Oh, yeah, Alison. What's up?

Ben is humping Jason's head.

              JONAH
   She like-a the way your dick tastes.

              ALISON
         (into the phone)
   I actually was just wondering if maybe
   you, wanted to get together, like
   tomorrow night?

              BEN
         (into the phone)
   I've been meaning to call you so we could
   hook up again. You know what I'm sayin'?

              ALISON
         (into the phone)
   Let's meet up maybe tomorrow night? You
   wanna just grab some dinner?

              BEN
         (into the phone)
   Why not? Meeting of minds sounds good.
   What do you say Geisha House, Hollywood,
   nine o'clock?

              ALISON
         (into the phone)
   Sure. That's cool. Can we make it more
   like six, though? I'd like to keep it
   early.

              BEN
         (into the phone)
   Six o'clock. Beat the rush. Yeah, leave
   more time for afterwards. Dessert. Sweet.

              ALISON
         (into the phone)
   Okay. I'll just meet you there, then, at
   six.

All the guys mime having sex with each other.

              BEN
         (into the phone)
   I'll see you there. Take care. Peace.

              ALISON
   Oh, shit.

              BEN
   I'm gonna get laid mother fuckers!

High fives all around for Ben and the roommates.

INT. GEISHA HOUSE - NIGHT

Ben and Alison sit at a table in the crowded restaurant.

                    BEN
          Nice place, huh?

                    ALISON
          It's really nice.

                    BEN
          Sorry it took so long to get a table. I
          didn't realize you needed a reservation.

          That's okay.

                    BEN
          You look very pretty, though.

                    ALISON
          Thanks. Yeah, I just thought, I don't
          know, I thought maybe it'd be cool to
          hang out a little bit and... We didn't
          really get to talk much last time so I
          thought--

                    BEN
          That we didn't.

                    ALISON
          I thought maybe we'd just talk and get to
          know each other...better.

                    BEN
          Cool. Okay, I'll start. I'm Canadian.

                    ALISON
          That's cool.

                    BEN
          From Vancouver. I live here illegally,
          actually. Don't tell anyone. But it works
          out in my advantage, ultimately, 'cause I
          don't have to pay any taxes. So
          financially that's helpful 'cause I don't
          have a lot of money. I'm not poor or
          anything but I eat a lot of spaghetti.

                    ALISON
          So the web page is it just something that
          you guys do for fun? Do you have a real
          job?

                    BEN
          Well, that is our job.

                    ALISON
          Oh.

                    BEN
          We don't technically get money for the
          hours we put in, but it is our job.

                    ALISON
          So, how do you...?

                    BEN
How do I pay rent and shit?

                    ALISON
Right.

                    BEN
When I was in high school, I got ran over
by a postal truck.

                    ALISON
Oh, my God.

                    BEN
It was my foot more than anything. But, I
got fourteen grand from the British
Columbia government.

                    ALISON
Right.

                    BEN
And that really lasted me until now. It's
been almost ten years. I have like nine
hundred bucks left. So that should last
me for I'm not a mathematician, but like
another two years or some shit...I think.

                    ALISON
Yeah. So, I have something I really need
to tell you. It's kind of why I called
you. Here it goes. I'm pregnant.

                    BEN
Fuck off.

                    ALISON
What?

                    BEN
What?

                    ALISON
I'm pregnant...?

                    BEN
With emotion?

                    ALISON
With a baby. You're the father.

                    BEN
I'm the father.

                    ALISON
Yes!

                    BEN
How the fuck could this happen?

                    ALISON
I don't know. I thought you were wearing
a condom.

                    BEN
No.

                    ALISON
What?

                    BEN
I wasn't.

                    ALISON
Why not?

                    BEN
Because you told me not to.

                    ALISON
What are you talking about?

                    BEN
What am I talking about? You told me not
to.

                    ALISON
I did not tell you not to wear a condom.

                    BEN
Here's what happened, okay? I will give
you a play-by-play of my memory. I almost
had the condom on my dick. It was on the
cusp and then you said, "Just do it,
already."

                    ALISON
I didn't mean do it without a condom. I
mean "do it" like "hurry up," like "get
fucking going!"

                    BEN
Well, I assumed you were wearing a patch,
or like a dental dam or one of those
fuckin' butterfly clips or something like
that.

                    ALISON
What the hell is a dental dam?

                    BEN
It's like Saran Wrap! It's disgusting,
okay? But I thought you had one. Why the
fuck didn't you stop me once we started?

                    ALISON
Oh, my God! I don't know! I couldn't tell
that you didn't have one on! Obviously, I
was drunk!

                    BEN
Was your vagina drunk? Did you think it's
the thinnest condom on earth I have on?
I'm a fuckin' inventor? I made a dick-
skin condom? He hollowed out a penis and
put it on? What the fuck?!

                    ALISON
You are unbelievable.

                    BEN
Okay, you know what? Maybe, I've reacted
unfavorably. So what happens now? I don't
know how this works.

                    ALISON
I am going to the doctor next week...and
I thought you could come with me to the
gynecologist.

                    BEN
So you haven't seen him, though?

                    ALISON
No.

                    BEN
So you don't know if you're pregnant.

                    ALISON
Well, I'm not a hundred percent sure.

                    BEN
You're not a hundred percent sure. I bet
you're not pregnant.

INT. DOCTOR'S OFFICE, WAITING ROOM - DAY

Ben and Alison sit in the crowded waiting room.

                    DR. PELLAGRINO'S NURSE
Alison Scott?

                    ALISON
Yeah, yeah.
     (to Ben)
Come on.

                    BEN
I'm supposed to go?

                    ALISON
Yes.

INT. DOCTOR'S OFFICE, EXAMINATION ROOM

Alison is in a gown on the table. Ben stands by looking at
the diagrams on the wall.

DR. PELLAGRINO enters.

                    DR. PELLAGRINO
Hello. My name is Thomas Pellagrino.

                    BEN
I'm Ben Stone.

                    DR. PELLAGRINO
Hi, there, champ. And you must be
Debbie's sister...Alice.

                    ALISON
Alison.

                    DR. PELLAGRINO
Hi. How are ya?

                    ALISON
Good.

                    DR. PELLAGRINO
          So, what can I help you with today,
          Mister and Mrs. Stone?

                    ALISON
          I took a home pregnancy test and it said
          I was pregnant, so here we are.

                    DR. PELLAGRINO
          Let's have a look. Legs up.

Alison puts her legs up and leans back.

                    BEN
          Nice office.

                    DR. PELLAGRINO
          Thank you.

Dr. Pellagrino examines Alison's genital area.

                    DR. PELLAGRINO(cont'd)
          Well, you do look a lot like your sister.

Dr. Pellagrino picks up a long cone shaped device.

                    DR. PELLAGRINO(cont'd)
          This is gonna be cold.

               (to Ben)
          And you're next. I'm just kidding.

Dr. Pellagrino looks at Ben and shrugs like saying "this is
just part of the job" as he puts the cone device inside
Alison.

                    DR. PELLAGRINO (cont'd)
          There's the cervix. And the uterus. See
          that? That dark sac there, that's the
          amniotic sac. And right there, in the
          middle is the embryo. Do you see that
          flicker? You know what that is? That's
          the heartbeat. Yeah, it looks like you
          are pregnant. About eight or nine weeks,
          I'd say. Congratulations.

Alison points to the monitor.

                    ALISON
          That, that's it?

                    DR. PELLAGRINO
          Yep. Take good care of it. Now the fun
          part starts. Let me make a picture for
          ya, huh? That'll be fun.

Alison begins to CRY.

                    DR. PELLAGRINO (cont'd)
          Well, I'll meet ya in my office. I'll
          give ya a little time alone, there.

Alison continues to cry. Ben stands by SILENTLY, stunned.

                    BEN
          Oh, God. It's okay.

INT. BEN'S HOUSE - NIGHT

All the roommates and Ben sit around passing a bong.

                JONAH
I can't fuckin' believe you didn't wear a
bag! Who does that?!

                JASON
Why did we go to Costco and buy a year's
supply of condoms if you weren't gonna
use 'em, man?

                JONAH
I can't believe you did this. You fucked
everything up.

                JASON
Look, the real point is not to get
yourself in this position. That's what
you have to realize. You gotta know all
the tricks. Like, for example, if a
woman's on top, she can't get pregnant.
It's just gravity.

                JONAH
Everyone knows that.

                JASON
What goes up must come down.

                JAY
I think it's awesome that you're gonna
have a kid, man. Think of it like this.
It's just an excuse to play with all your
old toys again.

                JONAH
You know what I think you should do? Take
care of it.

                JAY
Tell me you don't want him to get an "A
word."

                JONAH
Yes, I do, and I won't say it for little
Baby Ears over there, but it rhymes with
"shmish-mortion." I'm just saying -- hold
on Jay, cover your ears -- you should get
a "shmish-morshmion" at the "shmish-
morshmion" clinic.

                JAY
Ben, you cannot let these monsters have
any part of your child's life. All right?
I'm gonna be there to rear your child.

                JASON
You hear that, Ben? Don't let him near
the kid. He wants to rear your child!

Ben gets up and leaves the room.

                JONAH
Aw, Ben. Ben, come on, man.

> JASON
> I'm just kidding you.

> JAY
> Oh, great. Now he's upset.

> JASON
> I won't let him do it.

INT. RESTAURANT - DAY

Alison and her mother, BETTY, sit over lunch.

> BETTY
> Alison, just take care of it. Take care
> of it. Move on. What's gonna happen with
> your career? Or how, how are you gonna
> tell them?

> ALISON
> Well, I'm not gonna tell them for a
> while. I have a while before I have to
> say anything.

> BETTY
> How could you not tell them?

> ALISON
> Well, they're not gonna know. I mean, I'm
> only gonna start to show when I'm like, I
> don't know, six months or something.
> Seven months.

> BETTY
> Three months.

> ALISON
> No.

> BETTY
> Three months. Fat in the face, jowls, fat
> ass.

> ALISON
> Debbie didn't get fat.

> BETTY
> Debbie is a freak of nature.

> ALISON
> Mom, you know, it's important to me that
> you be supportive.

> BETTY
> I cannot be supportive of this. This is a
> mistake. This is a big, big mistake. Now
> think about your stepsister. Now, you
> remember what happened with her? She had
> the same situation as you and she had it
> taken care of. And you know what? Now she
> has a real baby. Honey, this is not the
> time.

INT. DINER - DAY

Ben and his father, HARRIS, sit at a table over lunch.

                    HARRIS
I'm gonna be a grandfather.

                    BEN
You happy about that?

                    HARRIS
Absolutely. Delighted.

                    BEN
This is a disaster.

                    HARRIS
No, this is not a disaster.

                    BEN
It is, you know?

                    HARRIS
An earthquake is a disaster. Your
grandmother having Alzheimer's so bad she
doesn't even know who the fuck I am,
that's a disaster. This is a good thing.
This is a blessing.

                    BEN
I had a vision for how my life would go
and this definitely is not it.

                    HARRIS
Wait. Are you living your vision right
now?

                    BEN
I am kinda living my vision, yeah.

                    HARRIS
Well, that is sad, I'm telling you. Life
doesn't care about your vision. Okay?

                    BEN
Okay.

                    HARRIS
Stuff happens. You just got to deal with
it. Roll with it. That's the beauty of it
all.

                    BEN
I just don't get how I tell the kid not
to do drugs when I do drugs. I'll feel
like a hypocrite.

                    HARRIS
Well you remember what I told you? When
you were a teenager?

                    BEN
What did you say?

                    HARRIS
I said, "No pill, no powders."

                    BEN
That's right, that's right.

                    HARRIS
Right. If it grows in the ground, it's
probably okay.

                    BEN
I guess it worked. You told me not to
smoke pot all those years. And then I
found out you were smoking pot that whole
time.

                    HARRIS
Not the *whole* time. Just in the evenings
and all day every weekend. Not that much.

                    BEN
Honestly, though, when you look at me, do
you not think at all, like, you know, if
he just never existed, I would have
avoided a massive heap of trouble? You
know?

                    HARRIS
Absolutely not. I love you totally and
completely. You're the best thing that
ever happened to me.

                    BEN
I'm the best thing that ever happened to
you?

                    HARRIS
Yeah.

                    BEN
Now I just feel bad for you.

INT. ALISON'S GUEST HOUSE - NIGHT

Alison dials the phone.

INT. BEN'S HOUSE, BEN'S BEDROOM - CONTINUOUS

Ben picks up.

INTERCUT:

                    BEN
Hello?

                    ALISON
Hi, Ben?

                    BEN
Hey Alison, how's it goin'?

                    ALISON
Good, good. You know, I was just calling
to, let you know that, I've decided to
keep the baby.That's what's happening
with that.

                    BEN
Good. That's good. That's what I was
hoping you'd do. So, awesome.

                    ALISON
          Yeah, yeah, it is good.

                    BEN
          I know we didn't plan this and neither of
          us really thought it was gonna happen but
          life is like that, you know? You can't
          plan for it and even if we did, life
          doesn't care about your plans,
          necessarily, and you just kinda have to
          go with the flow and I just know my job
          is to just support you in whatever it is
          you wanna do. I'm in, so whatever you
          wanna do, I'm gonna do.

Alison WEEPS softly into the phone.

                    BEN(cont'd)
          I'm on board. Yaaay.

                    ALISON
          I really appreciate you saying that.

                    BEN
          No problem. I'll tell you, maybe if you
          could help me by telling me, like one
          thing that I am supposed to do, then that
          would be good, 'cause I literally have no
          idea whatsoever.

                    ALISON
          I have no idea either.

                    BEN
          Do you want to, like, get together and
          talk about it or something like that?

                    ALISON
          Yeah, sure.

                    BEN
          Like a date? I mean...

                    ALISON
          Yeah.

EXT. BEN'S HOUSE

Alison drives up to Ben's House.

INT. BEN'S HOUSE

Alison KNOCKS on the door and Ben answers.

                    BEN
          Hey

                    ALISON
          Hi.

                    BEN
          You look beautiful.

                    ALISON
          Thank you.

                              BEN
               No problem. Come on in.

          Ben leads Alison into the living room where the rest of the
          roommates are hanging out.

                              BEN (cont'd)
               Everyone, this is Alison.

                              ALISON
               Hi.

                              JASON
               Ally. Hey. Jason. I'm sure you remember.

                              ALISON
               Yes.

                              JASON
               You look beautiful.

                              ALISON
               Thank you.

                              JASON
               Your body's responding really well to the
               pregnancy.

                              ALISON
               Thank you.

                              JASON
               It's amazing how fast the milk arrives.
               How's your sis?

                              ALISON
               She's good.

                              JASON
               Oh, good. Tell her "What's up" for me.

                              ALISON
               Okay.

                              JASON
               All right, I'm gonna go make a protein
               shake.

                              BEN
               And this, uh, beautiful young man is
               Jonah.

                              ALISON
               Hi.

                              JONAH
               Hey.

                              BEN
               Okay, that's Martin and Jodi over there.

                              ALISON
               Hi.

                    BEN
          I'm gonna grab my shirt. Just take a seat
          if you want.

Ben exits. Jonah is watching the lesbian sex scene in "Wild
Things."

                    JONAH
          Just another day at the office. Do you
          have any acting experience?

                    ALISON
          No.

                    MARTIN
          How's it goin'? You wanna toke?

                    ALISON
          Eh, no. I'm good.

                    JODI
          Hi.

                    ALISON
          Hi.

                    JODI
          I'm Jodi.

                    ALISON
          Yeah, hi.

                    JODI
          I heard you were pregnant.

                    ALISON
          Mm-hm.

                    JODI
          Oh, aren't you scared? The way it's gonna
          come out of your...It's gonna hurt a lot
          I bet. Your vagina...That's so sick.

                    ALISON
          I don't know.

                    JODI
          Are you hungry?

                    ALISON
          I'm okay right now. Thank you.

                    JODI
          You must be angry at the baby whenever it
          steals your food, huh? "Oh it's mine, not
          yours." But, you know... Because you're
          family, you got to share.

                    ALISON
          Right.

Jay enters the room in a towel after a shower.

                         JAY
          Man, my balls are shaved. My pubes are
          trimmed. I'm ready to fuckin' rock this
          shit.

                         JONAH
          What the fuck, man?! If I go in there and
          see fuckin' pubes sprinkled on the toilet
          seat, I'm gonna fuckin' lose my mind!
          Last time I went to the bathroom, Jay, I
          took a shit and my shit looked like a
          fuckin' stuffed animal!

                         JAY
          You're embarrassing me in company!

                         JONAH
          You embarrass yourself!

                         JAY
          Oh, great. I hope you have a great
          evening!

Jay exits. Ben enters in his new shirt.

                         BEN
          All right. Let's go. See you guys later.

EXT. MICELLI'S RESTAURANT

Establishing shot.

INT. MICELLI'S RESTAURANT

Alison and Ben sit in a booth over appetizers.

                         ALISON
          The funny thing is I really had never
          even thought about having a baby.

                         BEN
          Yeah.

                         ALISON
          If this hadn't happened, I don't think I
          would have wanted to have a baby for,
          like, I don't know, at least ten years.

                         BEN
          At least! God, honestly, I just got used
          to the notion that someone would even
          have sex with me. I didn't think this
          would happen.

EXT. JACADI, BABY CLOTHING STORE - NIGHT

Establishing shot.

INT. JACADI, BABY CLOTHING STORE

Ben puts on a baby hat and holds a baby outfit in front of
him.

                    BEN
          Get ready. This will be coming out of you
          in seven months. This is exactly what our
          baby will look like.

                    ALISON
          It's a beautiful picture, Ben.

                    BEN
          It is. It's not bad.
             (in a French accent)
          Hello, Mommy. Our baby's gonna be French
          Canadian. I like that.

                    ALISON
          With a little hint of Spanish.

                    BEN
          Exactly, I'm not good with accents.

EXT. BOOKSTORE - NIGHT

Establishing shot.

INT. BOOKSTORE

Ben and Alison browse the baby section.

                    BEN
          Baby books.

                    ALISON
          Awesome.

                    BEN
          "What to Expect When You're Expecting."

                    ALISON
          What can we expect?

                    BEN
          Well, you can't eat sushi. You can't
          smoke. You can't smoke marijuana. You
          can't smoke crack. And you can't jump on
          trampolines. This is basically a giant
          list of things you can't do.

                    ALISON
          It sounds thrilling.

                    BEN
          I'm gonna be sitting there on the
          trampoline smoking crack. And you're not
          gonna have anything to do. You're gonna
          be bored. But I can't wait to read these,
          honestly. I put these in front of my
          toilet, though, they'll be read by
          tomorrow morning. Do you want me to get
          you that?

                    ALISON
          Yeah, thank you.

                    BEN
          No problem. These are heavy.

EXT. MALL - NIGHT

Ben and Alison walk side-by-side carrying their purchases.
They both reach over and hold hands.

INT. DEBBIE AND PETE'S HOUSE, BATHROOM - NIGHT

Debbie and Pete get ready for bed at separate sinks.

>   PETE
> So what do you think? Should we have sex
> tonight?

>   DEBBIE
> Ugh. Sounds awful. I'm just really
> constipated. Do you really want to?

>   PETE
> Well, *now*.

>   DEBBIE
> Shut up.

>   PETE
> That's pretty crazy how your sister's
> pregnant.

>   DEBBIE
> We have to help her.

>   PETE
> I think they'll be fine. They'll work
> it...Look at us. It happened to us.

>   DEBBIE
> We'll help her raise the baby.

>   PETE
> Well...fuck!

EXT. ALISON'S GUEST HOUSE

Establishing shot.

INT. ALISON'S GUEST HOUSE

Alison and Ben stand while kissing.

>   BEN
> At least we don't have to use a condom,
> you know?

Alison pulls away.

>   BEN (cont'd)
> But we can. I brought some just in case.
> I don't have V.D. or anything. I mean, I
> don't, I thought--

>   ALISON
> It's not that.

>   BEN
> It's just I thought we could get a
> little...fun out of your situation, you
> know?

                    ALISON
          Okay, first of all, it's not my
          situation. It's our situation.

                    BEN
          I know that.

                    ALISON
          And just because I'm pregnant, I'm not
          some ruined woman and all romance goes
          out the door.

                    BEN
          I'm sorry. I like you a lot. That's all
          this is.

                    ALISON
          I like you, too.

                    BEN
          Sweet.

                    ALISON
          A little, so far. I mean, we have seven
          months before the baby comes. We don't
          have to rush it.

                    BEN
          Yeah.

                    ALISON
          We should really just try to get to know
          each other and...give this a real shot.
          You know? We got ourselves into this
          situation. We kind of have to.

                    BEN
          For the baby, right?

                    ALISON
          Exactly. Okay, if this was our second
          date, what would you do?

                    BEN
          B.J. If I'm just being honest. I told my
          roommates that I thought I was gonna get
          a B.J., so...

                    ALISON
          You know what? For the sake of getting to
          know one another, can you not talk like
          that?

                    BEN
          I can do that. I'm really nervous.

                    ALISON
          I'm nervous, too. I'm really nervous.

                    BEN
          Yeah.

Ben and Alison kiss.

                    ALISON
          You're a sweet guy, right?

                    BEN
          I think I am.

                    ALISON
          Don't fuck me over, okay?

                    BEN
          I wouldn't do that. Just so you know, I'm
          the guy girls fuck over. I'm that guy. So
          you don't fuck me over, okay?

                    ALISON
          Okay.

                    BEN
          I couldn't take it. I can't raise this
          baby alone.

Ben and Alison kiss.

EXT. DEBBIE AND PETE'S HOUSE - MORNING

Establishing shot.

INT. DEBBIE AND PETE'S HOUSE, KITCHEN

Debbie, Pete, Charlotte, Sadie, Alison and Ben eat breakfast
together.

                    CHARLOTTE
          Who's he?

                    BEN
          I'm Ben Stone.

                    ALISON
          He's my boyfriend.

                    PETE
          That's nice.

                    SADIE
          I never met him before.

                    ALISON
          He's a new boyfriend.

                    BEN
          But a boyfriend.

                    SADIE
          So he came over for breakfast because
          he's your new boyfriend?

                    DEBBIE
          He came from his house, drove over to our
          house because he thought it would be fun
          to have breakfast with us, so he drove
          his car from his house to our house to
          have breakfast.

                    PETE
          Because he likes breakfast so much.

                    CHARLOTTE
          I love breakfast.

                    BEN
You guys wanna hear something neat? We're
gonna have a baby together.

                    SADIE
What?

                    BEN
Yeah, a baby.

                    SADIE
Well, you're not married. Aren't you
supposed to be married to have a baby?

                    PETE
You don't have to be.

                    DEBBIE
But they should be because they love each
other and people who love each other get
married and have babies.

                    SADIE
Where do babies come from?

                    DEBBIE
Where do you think they come from?

                    SADIE
Well, I think a stork, he drops it down,
and then, a hole goes in your body and
there's blood everywhere, coming out of
your head, and then you push your belly-
button, and then your butt falls off and
then you hold you butt and you have to
dig and you find a little baby.

                    DEBBIE
That's exactly right.

EXT. DEBBIE AND PETE'S HOUSE, BACKYARD

Ben is in a playhouse with Sadie while Charlotte jumps on the
trampoline.

                    CHARLOTTE
Feed the teddy bear.

                    BEN
I feed your bear the grass? Know what
your bear would also like to do with some
grass? Smoke it.

Alison and Debbie watch Ben and the kids from the patio.

                    ALISON
         (to Debbie)
What do you think of him? He's funny,
right?

Ben throws the bear's bowl.

                    BEN
Fetch. All right, bring it back.

                              DEBBIE
                         (to Alison)
                    He's playing fetch with my kids. He's
                    treating my kids like they're dogs.

                              ALISON
                         (to Debbie)
                    No's he not.

Ben throws the bear this time.

                              BEN
                    Go get it! Fetch!

                              DEBBIE
                         (to Alison)
                    Plays fetch with the kids.

                              BEN
                    All right!

                              ALISON
                         (to Debbie)
                    He's trying. He's making an effort.

                              CHARLOTTE
                    I don't wanna play this anymore.

                              BEN
                    Bring it back.

                              DEBBIE
                         (to Alison)
                    He's overweight. Where does that end? How
                    old is he?

                              ALISON
                         (to Debbie)
                    Twenty-three.

                              DEBBIE
                         (to Alison)
                    Looks thirty-three. He can barely get in
                    and out of that little house. Imagine how
                    much bigger he's going to get.

Ben tries to exit the playhouse but gets stuck a couple
times.

                              DEBBIE (cont'd)
                    That means he has bad genes. Your kid is
                    going to be overweight.
                              ALISON
                    Shit.

                              BEN
                    I'm gonna get you!

Ben chases the girls on top of the trampoline.

                              BEN (cont'd)
                    I'm gonna get you! Whoa!

Ben falls off the trampoline onto the grass. The kids love
it.

                    ALISON
              (to Debbie)
          Just give him a break.

                    DEBBIE
              (to Alison)
          Okay, I'll try.

Charlotte pegs a beach ball at Ben's head.

EXT. PLAYGROUND - DAY

Ben and Pete sit while Charlotte and Sadie blow bubbles.

                    BEN
          They seem to love bubbles.

                    PETE
          They go ape-shit over bubbles.

                    BEN
          They're really going ape-shit.

                    PETE
          That's an incredible thing about a child.
          What's so great about bubbles?

                    BEN
          They float. You can pop them. I mean, I
          get it. I get it.

                    PETE
          I wish I liked anything as much as my
          kids like bubbles.

                    BEN
          That's sad.

                    PETE
          It's totally sad. Their smiling faces
          just point out your inability to enjoy
          anything.

                    BEN
          Am I going to be okay, man?

                    PETE
          Who knows? Is anybody okay? I'm not okay.
          You're asking the wrong guy. Just don't
          ask me to lend you any money, you know?

                    BEN
          Can I just have some?

                    PETE
          No.

EXT. BEN'S HOUSE - DAY

Jason and Jonah play ping-pong while the rest of the
roommates, including Ben, watch.

                    JASON
          I have fifteen years of tennis lessons.

                    JONAH
And twelve years of sucking dick lessons.

              JAY
     (to Ben)
So?

              BEN
I can't ref the next games, by the way. I
got to go meet gynecologists with Alison.
She doesn't like her gynecologist.

              JAY
You think she likes you?

              BEN
She's trying to.

              JAY
She's entertaining the idea of liking
you.

              BEN
Exactly. I'll take that.

              JAY
Well, see she's bringing you to the
gynechiatrist. She must like you.

              BEN
That's pretty good, I think.

              JASON
You know who I'd like to get pregnant is
that Felicity Huffman, man. Ever since
"Transamerica," I can't get her out of my
mind.

              BEN
Guys, I hate to crack the whip, but it's
kind of, uh, business meeting time. I
need moolah. When do you think we can
launch this site?

              JAY
Geez.

              JONAH
You can't rush this. You know what
happens to these sites when they go up
and they don't function well? They die.

              BEN
Seriously, guys, let's say I want to
launch today. Let's start... let's use
that as a jumping off point. Let's make
this happen. What can we do?

              JONAH
Look, man, I didn't go to Yale so I could
work twelve hours a day.

              JASON
I thought you went to Santa Monica City
College.

> JONAH
> I went where I went, Jason.

> BEN
> I'm not asking you to work twelve hours a
> day. I mean, you guys watch movies
> without nudity in them.

> JASON
> I'll tell you what, man. We could
> probably get it online in three months.

> BEN
> Thank you. Yes! Three months.

> JONAH
> Come on, Jason!

Jason serves the ball and Jonah hits it as hard as he can to
win the game.

> JONAH (cont'd)
> Fuck off!

> JASON
> Yeah, well, you still have a little dick,
> Cartman.

EXT. TOWN STREET - DAY

Ben and Alison drive to the gynecologist.

INT. DOCTOR'S OFFICE

Alison is on the examination table while DR. KUNI examines
her.

> DR. KUNI
> Do you smoke cigarettes?

> ALISON
> No.

> DR. KUNI
> Do you smoke cigarettes?

> ALISON
> I have on occasion.

> DR. KUNI
> On occasion? When? When was the last time
> you had one cig? You know, on, you know,
> a little...I need to know or I will not
> be your doctor.

INT. GYM

Ben and Alison are in a spin class. Ben is sweating
profusely.

> ALISON
> How ya doing?

> BEN
> I'm breathing like James Gandolfini over
> here.

A person next to them peddles extremely fast.

>   BEN (cont'd)
>   (to nearby athlete)
>   Slow down, man. You're making me look
>   like a jackass.

INT. DOCTOR'S OFFICE

Alison is on the table with her legs up while a YOUNG DOCTOR examines her. Ben sits by Alison.

>   YOUNG DOCTOR
>   How long you kids been married?

>   BEN
>   We're not.

>   ALISON
>   No.

>   YOUNG DOCTOR
>   You're single?

>   BEN
>   She's not single. She's just not married.

>   YOUNG DOCTOR
>   Are you two together?

Alison and Ben share a look of disbelief that the doctor is hitting on her.

INT. BEN'S HOUSE, KITCHEN - DAY

Jodi and Alison are in the kitchen, cutting vegetables.

>   JODI
>   Hey, you wanna trade boyfriends? Just
>   kidding. Kind of.

INT. DOCTOR'S OFFICE

Alison is on the table while a FEMALE DOCTOR examines her. Ben watched on.

>   FEMALE DOCTOR
>   Wow. That is not your vagina. That's your
>   asshole. That happens about five times a
>   day.

INT. BEN'S HOUSE

Alison and Ben sit on the couch. The rest of the roommates are all suited up for paintball.

>   JAY
>   Are you sure you don't want to come paint-
>   balling?

>   BEN
>   Have fun, guys. Seriously, watch the
>   eyes.

>   JAY
>   All right.

                         JASON
          See ya, Ally.

                         JONAH
          Peace.

                         JAY
          Bye.

Alison looks at Ben.

                         BEN
          I don't want to go. I swear to God. I
          want to see "Breathless" at the LACMA.

INT. BEN'S HOUSE - DAY

Alison is watching a movie during a scene with a topless
woman.

                         ALISON
          Boobs! Boobs! Boobs!

Ben runs in.

                         BEN
          Hold on, pause it, pause it, pause it.

                         ALISON
          Boobs and bush.

Ben hops on the couch the log the scene for the website.

                         ALISON (cont'd)
          Good boobs.

                         BEN
          Those are good ones! We're like thirty-
          five seconds in.

                         ALISON
          Right over the beginning credits.

                         BEN
          Nice. Credit bush. You never get opening-
          credit bush.

                         ALISON
          I know. That's so crazy.

EXT. DEBBIE'S HOUSE, POOL - DAY

Alison sits on the side as Ben plays with Charlotte and Sadie
in the pool.

                         BEN
          You got me. You got me.

INT. DOCTOR'S OFFICE - DAY

Ben and Alison sit across the desk from DR. HOWARD.

                         ALISON
          How many doctors are there in your
          practice?
                         (MORE)

                    ALISON (cont'd)
Just because I'm sort of looking for a
more personal experience. I want to make
sure that you're my doctor on the day
and...

                    DR. HOWARD
I understand. We have three other doctors
in the practice but I'm your man, okay? I
don't take vacations. I hate Hawaii. I
went to the Caribbean when I was fourteen
and I'm never going back.

                    ALISON
I feel really good about this.

    (to Ben)
I think we found our doctor.

                    BEN
Really?

                    ALISON
Yeah.

                    BEN
Oh, my God. Are you serious right now?

                    DR. HOWARD
You look relieved.

                    BEN
I am very relieved.

                    DR. HOWARD
All right.

                    BEN
I can't imagine meeting any more of you
people.

                    ALISON
You're being dramatic. We didn't meet
that many.

CARD: 16 WEEKS.

INT. E ENTERTAINMENT TELEVISION STUDIO

Alison is being measured by the WARDROBE LADY.

                    WARDROBE LADY
Ooh. Do they know?

                    ALISON
Pardon?

                    WARDROBE LADY
The belly.

                    ALISON
The doughnuts, they call to me.

                    WARDROBE LADY
You're--

Jill walks by.

                         JILL
         Hey, Alison!

                         ALISON
         Hi.

                         JILL
         Great job.

                         ALISON
         Thanks.

                         JILL
              (to herself)
         For you.

                         WARDROBE LADY
         You're pregnant aren't you?

                         ALISON
         What?

                         WARDROBE LADY
         I mean, you've put on like eight pounds,
         nine. It's all in your uterus.

                         ALISON
         Oh, shit. I haven't told them. Do you
         think they're gonna be mad? I'm really
         chickening out about this.

                         WARDROBE LADY
         It's okay. We can hide this. We'll dress
         you in black and we'll emphasize your
         boobs.

                         ALISON
         Awesome.

                         WARDROBE LADY
         Your boobs are going to be big. And then
         they're going to be like scary big. But
         then they'll go down. And then they'll
         stay down.

                         ALISON
         Just don't say anything, okay? Please
         don't say anything.

                         WARDROBE LADY
         I won't. Just tell them. They'll be cool.
         Everybody loves somebody pregnant.

EXT. DEBBIE AND PETE'S HOUSE - DAY

Establishing shot.

INT. DEBBIE AND PETE'S HOUSE, LIVING ROOM

Debbie and Pete use a laptop. Ben enters.

                         DEBBIE
         Ooh. Did you see this sex offender
         website? These are all the sex offenders
         in our neighborhood.

Debbie points to the screen which has a map with red dots spread over it.

                    PETE
          Looks like your computer has chicken pox.

                    DEBBIE
          Those are sex offenders. These people
          live in our neighborhood.

                    PETE
          We'll skip their houses when we're trick
          or treating. What do you want me to do?
          Form a posse?
                    (to Ben)
          Got your six-shooter on ya? I got my
          lynching rope.

                    DEBBIE
          You shouldn't take it so lightly.

                    PETE
          I don't take it lightly. I'm not going to
          go over to any of these people's houses
          and say, "Hey, you mind? Can you baby
          sit?"

                    DEBBIE
          If I didn't care about these things, you
          wouldn't care about anything. Care more.

                    PETE
          You're so concerned with stuff, like
          don't get them vaccinated, don't let them
          eat fish. There's mercury in the water.
          Jesus, how much "Dateline NBC" can you
          watch?

                    DEBBIE
          I know we're supposed to be nice with
          each other right now, but I'm having a
          really hard time. I'm struggling with it
          right now.

                    PETE
          What am I doing?

                    DEBBIE
          Because I want to rip your fucking head
          off because you're so fucking stupid!
          This is scary.

                    DEBBIE (cont'd)
          These are our children. You fucking
          dipshit!

                    PETE
          I literally am at a point where I don't
          know what I can say.

                    DEBBIE
          So I'm the bad guy because I'm trying to
          protect our kids from child molesters and
          mercury? And you're cool because you
          don't give a shit?

                    PETE
          Yeah.

                    DEBBIE
          Yeah? Is that it?

                    PETE
          Pretty much.

                    DEBBIE
          God, you're an asshole.

                    PETE
          Don't do this in front of Ben.

                    DEBBIE
          I don't give a shit about Ben.

                    PETE
          Sorry, Ben.

                    BEN
          It's okay. I didn't think she did,
          anyway.

Alison enters.

                    ALISON
          Okay, come on! Let's go.

                    PETE
          I can't go. This band is doing a showcase
          out in the Valley. I got to go.

                    DEBBIE
          It's Saturday.

                    PETE
          I got to go.

INT. BABY CLOTHES AND ACCESSORIES STORE

Debbie and Alison are browsing the baby furniture. Ben trails
behind.

                    DEBBIE
          You don't want to know the sex of the
          baby? That's no fun.

                    ALISON
          Ben knows, but I've sworn him to secrecy.

                    DEBBIE
          I'll get it out of him.

Ben looks at Baby Bjorn baby carriers. He brings one to
Alison.

                    BEN
          Hey. Think we'll ever be as happy as Baby
          Bjorn couple is?

                    ALISON
          We are that happy.

                    BEN
          Yeah. You look happy.

                    ALISON
          Which is awesome. Because I never like
          guys like you. It's great.

                    BEN
          You keep saying that. I know.

Alison and Ben walk over to Debbie who is in front of a crib.

                    DEBBIE
          This is it. This is perfect.

                    BEN
          Nice.

Ben looks at the price tag.

                    BEN (cont'd)
          Holy shit, it's fourteen hundred bucks.

                    ALISON
              (to Debbie)
          We can just borrow yours. Is that okay?

                    DEBBIE
          No. You need your own crib.

                    BEN
          There's one of these in an alley behind
          my house. We could just grab that. Just
          rub Purell all over it.

                    DEBBIE
          You know what? Let me buy it. I need to
          get you a baby present anyway, and I
          would love to get it for you.

                    ALISON
          No.

                    DEBBIE
          I'm serious. I want to.

                    ALISON
          No. It's too much.

                    BEN
              (whispering to Alison)
          Shh. Yes. We'll take it obviously. I mean
          don't insult the woman. She wants to get
          us a gift.

                    DEBBIE
          Right.

                    BEN
          Want to buy me some new clothes? What
          else can I squeeze out of you? XBOX360,
          XBOX360.

EXT. BABY CLOTHES AND ACCESSORIES STORE

Alison and Ben are carrying clothes to the car. Alison stops
in her tracks when she sees a group of two young women and a
man approaching.

                    ALISON
          It's so hot in the Valley.

                    GIRL #1
          Hey!

                    GIRL #2
          Oh, my God!

                    ALISON
          Oh, shit.

                    GIRL #1
          Alison!

                    ALISON
          Hi!

                    GIRL #2
          Oh, it's so good to see you.

                    ALISON
          You too. Oh, my God.

                    GIRL #2
          We've been watching you on E! It's the
          coolest thing.

                    ALISON
          Yeah, it's been super-exciting, just
          crazy busy. I'm so sorry I haven't
          called.

                    GIRL #2
          Oh, it's fine.
            (to Ben)
          Hi, I'm Ashley.

                    ALISON
          This is my friend, Ben.

                    BEN
          I'm Ben.

                    GIRL #2
          I went to school with Alison.

                    GIRL #1
          So, okay, so is Debbie having another
          baby?

                    BEN
          No. Alison is.

                    GIRL #2
          What?! I just saw you a couple months
          ago. You're pregnant?

                    ALISON
          It was a big surprise.

                    BEN
It's a really funny story, actually, if
you guys, if you got a second to hear it.

                    ALISON
It's not really funny.

                    GIRL #1
Tell us.

                    ALISON
It's not funny.

                    BEN
Let them be the judge, okay? I think it's
funny.

                    ALISON
All right.

                    BEN
You know they say don't drink and drive?

                    GUY #1
Right.

                    BEN
Don't drink and bone!

                    GIRL #2
Wow.

EXT. RECORD STORE - DAY

Establishing shot.

INT. RECORD STORE

Ben and Pete browse the records.

                    BEN
Yeah, she was acting weird and I really
think it's just because I haven't made an
honest woman out of her. She's carrying
my bastard child. No one wants that.

                    PETE
That's what I did. I married Debbie when
she got pregnant.

                    BEN
You think she's, like, hiding me? Like,
she's, like, embarrassed by me or
something like that?

                    PETE
Probably. I'd hide you.

                    BEN
How much do wedding rings cost?

                    PETE
It really depends, you know? I think
you're supposed to spend three months pay
on a ring.

                    BEN
That'll be easy. I don't make any money.

                    PETE
Really? I thought there was a lot of
money in porn.

                    BEN
God, it's not porn? All we do is we show
you what nude scenes are in what movies.

                    PETE
Like Mister Skin?

                    BEN
Who's Mister Skin?

                    PETE
Dude, Mister Skin.

Pete imitates the Mister Skin logo smile.

INT. BEN'S HOUSE - DAY

Ben and the roommates look at the Mister Skin website.

                    JONAH
We've wasted fourteen months of our
lives.

                    BEN
This is exactly the same as our site. How
the fuck did this happen?

                    JONAH
Mister Skin! That's even a better name
than ours!

                    MARTIN
Well, fuck me in the beard.

                    JASON
Dude, they got the top ten group shower
scenes! Why didn't you think of that,
Jay!

                    JAY
Don't put this on me!

                    BEN
God damn it!

                    MARTIN
Well shit. I saw it online at one point,
but I guess I didn't connect the dots.

                    JONAH
What are we gonna do now?

                    BEN
All we need to do is think of a new,
better idea that no one else has thought
of already.

                    JASON
          "Spiderman Three" starts in eight
          minutes.

                    JONAH
          Shit. Don't worry. We'll figure it out.

Jonah, Jason and Martin exit. Ben and Jay sit at the desk.

                    BEN
          You know what? Just because this site
          exists doesn't mean ours won't work. Good
          things come in pairs.

                    JAY
          For sure.

                    BEN
          "Volcano," "Dante's Peak." "Deep Impact,"
          "Armageddon." "Wyatt Earp," "Tombstone."

                    JAY
          Panda Express, Yoshinoya Beef Bowl.

                    BEN
          Exactly. We can work together. This helps
          us, if anything.

                    JAY
          We're golden.

EXT. ALISON'S GUEST HOUSE - AFTERNOON

Establishing shot.

INT. ALISON'S GUEST HOUSE

Alison sits on the bed while Ben kneels in front of her.

                    BEN
          Alison, I'm sure this isn't how you
          pictured it being exactly and it's not
          how I wanted it. That is why I'm
          presenting you with this empty box. It's
          a promise, Alison. A promise that one day
          I will fill this with a ring that you
          deserve, a beautiful ring. I can't afford
          it yet. I've picked it out, though. It's
          at De Beers and it's really nice. So,
          basically, I'm asking you, will you marry
          me? Because I'm in love with you.

                    ALISON
          I love you too.

                    BEN
          Really? That's so nice to hear. That's
          the first time a girl's ever said that to
          me.

                    ALISON
          But here's the thing.

                    BEN
          There's a thing?

                    ALISON
          I don't really know yet what that love
          means. It's so new and it's so exciting.
          It's great. I don't know. We've only
          known each other for seventeen weeks.

                    BEN
          Look, I thought you felt weird that we're
          having a baby and we're not engaged. I'm
          going to get off my knee. It hurts.

Ben sits next to Alison on the bed.

                    ALISON
          I'm okay with that. We're just doing what
          we can. I don't want us to put any more
          pressure on ourselves than we have.

                    BEN
          That makes sense.

                    ALISON
          I didn't hurt your feelings, did I?

                    BEN
          No. I just wanted to do right by you. If
          you don't want to, that's totally cool.

                    ALISON
          I really do love you.

                    BEN
          I know. Thanks. You mentioned that. It's
          nice.

INT. DEBBIE AND PETE'S HOUSE, BEDROOM - NIGHT

Debbie and Alison eat ice cream in bed and watch TV.

                    ALISON
          Ben proposed to me. He did. It was really
          sweet. I feel a little bad. He was
          wearing this great button-down. He tucked
          it in. He got down on one knee. He didn't
          have an actual ring, though, just an
          empty box but he had this whole spiel
          about when he has the money, he'll buy me
          the ring I deserve.

                    DEBBIE
          The box was empty?

                    ALISON
          He can't afford a ring.

                    DEBBIE
          So he got down on one knee and gave you
          an empty box?

                    ALISON
          Yes.

                    DEBBIE
          I'm sorry.

                    ALISON
          Get over it. If you'd been there, you
          would have cried.

                    DEBBIE
          You need to train him. Oprah said that
          when two people meet they should point
          out each other's differences and flaws.

                    ALISON
          I thought you should love people for who
          they are.

                    DEBBIE
          You criticize them a lot, so they get so
          down on themselves they have to change.

                    ALISON
          You don't think that's naggy?

                    DEBBIE
          In the end, they thank you for it.

I/E DEBBIE'S CAR - DAY

Debbie drives Alison and the girls in her car.

                    DEBBIE
          You can't commit to him. You don't even
          know him. I don't even know Pete after
          ten years. I don't know what he's up to.
          He's miserable.

                    ALISON
          Why do you say that?

                    DEBBIE
          I think he's cheating on me. He's always
          going to business meetings at odd hours.
          Then I try to call him on his cell phone
          and he says he's in bad cell phone
          reception areas when he's in good
          reception areas.

                    ALISON
          Maybe he's working late. Maybe he's
          trying to sign a new band. I can't
          imagine Pete doing that.

                    DEBBIE
          There's no part of you that thinks maybe
          he's a dirty little scumbag?

                    ALISON
          No.

                    DEBBIE
          I think he might be.

INT. DEBBIE AND PETE'S HOUSE, OFFICE - DAY

Debbie installs software on the computer while Alison
watches.

                    DEBBIE
          "Memory Spy Web Memory Software. Locate
          history, files, websites visited, hidden
          downloads, e-mail history. Memory Spy."
          Let's see you hide from me now, little
          man.

Alison is disturbed by this whole ordeal.

CARD: 24 WEEKS LATER.

INT. FANCY RESTAURANT

Debbie, Pete, Alison and Ben eat dinner together.

                    PETE
          You're not going to tell them?

                    ALISON
          No. I don't have to. It's illegal for
          them to fire me over it. And I get three
          months maternity leave if I stay. So I'm
          not going to tell them.

                    DEBBIE
          Good plan.

                    PETE
          I like it.

                    BEN
          It's a good plan until her water breaks
          over Robert De Niro's shoes.
               (impersonating Robert De Niro)
          My shoes. There's baby goo on them.

                    PETE
               (impersonating Robert De Niro)
          These shoes? On these shoes? Did you puke
          on my shoes?

                    BEN
               (impersonating Robert De Niro)
          Is your water on my shoes?

                    PETE
               (back as Pete)
          Isn't it weird, though, when you have a
          kid and all your dreams and hopes go
          right out the window.

                    DEBBIE
          What changed for you? What went out the
          window? You do everything exactly the
          same.

                    PETE
          No, I love what I'm doing. But say before
          you're married with children you want to
          live in India for a year. You can do it.

                    DEBBIE
          You want to go to India? Go to India!
          Seriously.

                    PETE
          Do you want to go to India?

                    DEBBIE
          No. You can go.

                    BEN
          I get what he means. Honestly, when I
          found out about...

Ben motions towards Alison.

                    BEN (cont'd)
          ...I had this flash of me in a white Ford
          Bronco hauling ass for Canada. The
          chopper's taping it, and I bust through
          the border and I'm free! I kept thinking
          that.

Alison stares at Ben.

                    BEN (cont'd)
          It was a flash!

                    ALISON
          What do you mean?

                    BEN
          Don't look at me. We can talk about our
          fears here. If Doc Brown screeched up to
          you in the DeLorean and said, "Alison, I
          got the car here. What do you want to
          do?" No part of you would think, "Maybe
          I'll go back to that night and put a
          condom on Ben's dick?" You never got that
          flash?

                    ALISON
          No. What are you talking about?

                    PETE
          "Where we're going, we don't need roads."

                    BEN
          You wouldn't do that?

                    ALISON
          I don't know who Doc Brown is. What are
          you talking about?

                    BEN
          Doc Brown is Christopher Lloyd. He
          invented the DeLorean time machine.

                    PETE
          Everyone has a time machine image.

                    DEBBIE
          I have a really good idea. Why don't you
          two get in your time machine, go back in
          time and fuck each other?

                    PETE
          Who needs a time machine?

Ben holds up his drink.

                    BEN
          This is my time machine!

                    PETE
               (to Ben)
          I'll throw you in my DeLorean and gun it
          to 88.

                    BEN
               (to Pete)
          You are a funny motherfucker, man.

               (to Debbie)
          How can you fight with him? I just want
          to kiss his face. He's cute.

                    PETE
               (to Ben)
          I like the way you move.

                    BEN
          This is fun! We should do this more. This
          is the most fun I've had in a really long
          time.

EXT. BEN'S HOUSE - NIGHT

Establishing shot.

INT. BEN'S HOUSE, BEN'S BEDROOM

Ben and Alison are having sex. Ben is on top.

                    ALISON
          Come on, harder.

                    BEN
          I can't.

                    ALISON
          Why? Just do it deeper.

                    BEN
          I can't.

                    ALISON
          Why?

                    BEN
          I'll poke the baby if I go deeper.

                    ALISON
          Just do it!

                    BEN
          Please don't yell at me.

                    ALISON
          The doctor and Debbie said it's fine.
          Come on!

Ben stops.

                    BEN
          I'm sorry, can we change positions? I'm
          going to crush the baby.

                    ALISON
          That's ridiculous!

                    BEN
No, it's not. It has no shell.

                    ALISON
Millions of people have sex when they're
pregnant! It just works!

                    BEN
I weigh over 200 pounds.

                    ALISON
Just get over it.

                    BEN
I can't do it. Can you just get on top?
All I can see if our baby, poked in the
face by my penis.

                    ALISON
Trust me, you're not even close. Okay,
fine.

Alison moves on top. Alison abruptly stops.

                    ALISON (cont'd)
I can't do this. I can't focus like this.
I look disgusting from this angle. I can
feel you looking at my chins.

                    BEN
You look beautiful. Your chin looks so
skinny.

                    ALISON
And my boobs are all like, squishy and
they're flopping around. I can feel it
and it's distracting. It's all National
Geographic.

                    BEN
     (whispering)
Do you want to do it doggie style?

                    ALISON
No. I do not want you to fuck me like a
dog.

                    BEN
I'm not fucking you like a dog. It's
doggie style. It's just the style. I'm,
it's not like a dog. We don't have to go
outside or anything.

Ben and Alison lie down side by side, Ben is behind.

                    BEN (cont'd)
Here we go. Is it good?

                    ALISON
Yeah.

                    BEN
Should I go slower?

                    ALISON
Harder.

                    BEN
          Just tell me when you're close.

                    ALISON
          Just go harder.

                    BEN
          Okay.

                    ALISON
          Keep going!

Ben recoils.

                    BEN
          Oh, God. Oh, fuck!

                    ALISON
          What happened?

                    BEN
          The baby. It kicked my hand.

                    ALISON
          It always kicks.

                    BEN
          No, no, no, no, no.

                    ALISON
          It's fine.

                    BEN
          Not like this. No, this was a warning
          kick.

                    ALISON
          Just keep going.

                    BEN
          This was a bad kick.

                    ALISON
          It's fine! It's fine!

                    BEN
          Look. My dick must be like an inch away
          from its face and it's coming, just
          coming in at its face. What if it kicked
          because it didn't like it? I can't do
          that to our baby. That's the first thing
          it's going to see.

                    ALISON
          What are you talking about?

                    BEN
          It's having the baby between us, it just
          makes it weird. I'm sorry. It just freaks
          me out a bit. It's a little weird.

                    ALISON
          I have totally lost it now.

                    BEN
          You've totally lost it?

                    ALISON
        I've lost it.

                    BEN
        Okay.

                    ALISON
        Great, you know what? Just forget it.

Alison turns her back to Ben and gets settled to sleep.

                    ALISON (cont'd)
              (holding back tears)
        Don't worry. I won't make you do this
        again.

                    BEN
        Shit.

INT. BEN'S HOUSE, LIVING ROOM - NIGHT

Ben smokes his bong.

Suddenly, there is an earthquake.

INT. BEN'S HOUSE, BEN'S BEDROOM

Alison wakes up from the earthquake in a panic.

                    ALISON
        Ben?

INT. BEN'S HOUSE, LIVING ROOM

Ben stands up and tries to steady himself.

                    BEN
        Fuck me.

Jay runs through the room towards the front door.

                    JAY
        Oh my God! It's the Russians.

Martin carries Jodi out.

                    MARTIN
        Jodi! I'll protect you!

Ben clutches his bong and runs to the door. Alison runs to
the door as well.

                    ALISON
        Ben!

                    BEN
        Oh, my God! Oh, no! Oh, no!

EXT. BEN'S HOUSE - MOMENTS LATER

Jay, Martin, Alison, Jodi, Jonah, Jason and Ben stand on the
street. Jason is naked. Jonah's girlfriend ALEX is also
naked.

                        JAY
          That was horrible! That was so horrible.

                        JASON
          You're fine, man.

                        JAY
          When will it be light out?

                        JASON
          Take it easy.

                        JAY
          When will it be light out?

                        JASON
          Did anybody turn off the gas?

                        MARTIN
          I didn't do it.

                        JASON
          Oh, motherfucker.

Jason runs back to the house.

                        JONAH
          Martin, this is my friend, Alex. She's a
          pretty incredible person.

                        MARTIN
          Nice to meet you.

Martin holds out his hand to shake Alex's. She removes one
hand from covering her breast to shake his hand. Jonah
immediately covers her breast with his hand.

                        JONAH
          Whoa, whoa, whoa. Dude! Not cool, Martin.

                        MARTIN
          That's, that wasn't...

                        JONAH
          Hey, are you serious, Howard Hughes?

                        JODI
          What happened?

                        MARTIN
          Nothing. Nothing happened. Come on.

                        ALISON
            (to Ben)
          Where were you?

                        BEN
          Look, I forgot you were sleeping over.
          I'm sorry okay?

                        ALISON
          Yeah, because you were getting high off
          your huge bong. How am I supposed to be
          comfortable with the idea that you can
          take care of me and the baby if you are
          always getting high?

                         BEN
              You want me to stop smoking pot because
              there's an earthquake once every ten
              years? That makes no sense, Alison.
              You're being irrational. Just relax.
              We're all scared. Oh, shit, the cops.

A cop car rolls by. Ben throws his bong behind him and it
SHATTERS on the payment.

                         BEN (cont'd)
              California. Hey!

INT. BEN'S HOUSE, BEN'S BEDROOM

Ben and Alison sort through the debris of porn, trash and
weed among other things.

Alison finds Ben's bank statement that indicates he only has
only $117.13.

                         BEN
              You know it's times like this I'm glad I
              don't own nice things. It's a big mess,
              but there's only like fifty bucks worth
              of shit here. That's kind of the good
              thing. You know, my dad told me, "Don't
              move to Northridge." But you figure, what
              are the chances of that happening twice,
              you know?

Alison picks up a huge sword.

                         ALISON
              What is this?

                         BEN
              It's a ninja weapon. I hope this place
              doesn't get condemned. That would suck.

Alison finds a shopping bag with the baby books they bought.
None of them have been read. Alison sadly puts them back
without Ben noticing.

CARD: 28 WEEKS LATER.

INT. BEN'S HOUSE - DAY

Ben's phone RINGS.

                         BEN
              Hello?

INT. ALISON'S WORK

Alison is at her desk at work.

                         ALISON
              Hey it's me.

INTERCUT:

                         BEN
              You!

> ALISON
> Hi! So, listen. Will you do me a big
> favor? Debbie wants us to come over and
> have dinner tonight. She thinks Pete is
> cheating on her.

> BEN
> Really?

> ALISON
> Yeah. Well, she saw one of his e-mails
> and there's an address. Ugh.

> BEN
> Oh, man. I don't want to do that.

> ALISON
> Ben, come on.

> BEN
> He's not cheating on her.

> ALISON
> How do you know?

> BEN
> I just know.

> ALISON
> Are you sure?

> BEN
> I'm one hundred percent sure he's not
> cheating.

> ALISON
> Are you really?

> BEN
> No. It actually kind of makes sense that
> he would cheat.

> ALISON
> Why?

> BEN
> Because Debbie's a pain in the ass and
> Pete's awesome?

> ALISON
> Well, why don't you just come over then,
> and, we'll just diffuse the situation a
> little?

INT. DEBBIE AND PETE'S HOUSE, DINING ROOM - NIGHT

Alison, Ben, Pete and Debbie have dinner.

> PETE
> I'm just saying the music industry is
> different now. Steely Dan would never
> even have a chance.

> BEN
> Well, maybe it's because Steely Dan
> gargles my balls.

                    PETE
They're incredible.

                    BEN
They really aren't good, man.

                    PETE
Old Steely Dan.

                    BEN
If I ever listen to Steely Dan, I want
you to slice my head off with an Al
Jarreau LP.

                    PETE
I should get going. I'm supposed to see
this band tonight in Hollywood. Actually,
they're playing in Laurel Canyon, so I'll
call you because the reception's terrible
over there.

                    BEN
That's true.

                    PETE
And I don't want you to worry. I'm just
going to jump in the shower. It would be
terrible if I smelled worse than the
band.

                    DEBBIE
Okay. Have fun.

Ben exits.

                    BEN
You guys are crazy. He's acting totally
normal and hilarious.

EXT. FANTASY BASEBALL HOUSE - NIGHT

Debbie pulls up in front of the house in her car with Alison
and Ben.

                    BEN
           (to Alison)
She doesn't have a gun, does she?

                    ALISON
No. I don't think so.

                    BEN
Oh, great.

INT. FANTASY BASEBALL HOUSE

Debbie tries the front door, it's unlocked. They enter.

                    BEN
Looks like no one's home.

                    DEBBIE
Why was the door unlocked? Wait here.

                    BEN
I just feel bad for Pete.

                    ALISON
What?

                    BEN
I feel like this isn't a good way to get
caught cheating, it shouldn't be like
this.

                    ALISON
Well, maybe he should have thought of
that before he was cheating.

                    BEN
     (through a fake cough)
Pete!

                    ALISON
Stop it.

                    BEN
I coughed. What do you want from me?

Debbie checks upstairs.

                    DEBBIE
There's nobody up there.

                    BEN
Thank you.

                    DEBBIE
I guess I was wrong.

                    BEN
I told you. Can we get out of here,
please?

                    ALISON
Yeah, come on. Let's go.

A MURMUR comes from a far room.

                    DEBBIE
Did you hear that?

                    ALISON
What?

                    BEN
I didn't hear anything.

                    ALISON
Come on.

Debbie leads them into a room, where Pet sits with a lot of
GUYS dressed in baseball clothing.

                    FANTASY BASEBALL GUY #1
Ten seconds.

                    PETE
Carlos Delgado.

                    FANTASY BASEBALL GUY #2
Excellent choice. Too bad I got him three
rounds ago.

                    FANTASY BASEBALL GUY #1
You're still on the clock.

                    PETE
Oh shit!

                    FANTASY BASEBALL GUY #1
You gotta do something. We need a name
here.

                    PETE
Hideki Matsui.

                    FANTASY BASEBALL GUY #1
Ugh, you just took my whole outfield.

                    PETE
Sorry, Charlie.

                    DEBBIE
What is this?

                    PETE
Debbie.

                    DEBBIE
What the fuck is this?

                    PETE
It's our fantasy baseball draft.

                    FANTASY BASEBALL GUY #2
We said no wives.

                    DEBBIE
Your fantasy what?

                    PETE
It's, it's our draft...for fantasy
baseball. I told you all about this. Got
Matsui.

Debbie turns and walks out of the room.

                    PETE (cont'd)
Aw, shit.

                    FANTASY BASEBALL GUY #2
Hey, Pete, don't let the door hit you in
the vagina on the way out! Come on, who's
going?

EXT. FANTASY BASEBALL HOUSE

Pete and Debbie are in the driveway while Alison and Ben
watch from the street.

                    PETE
I should have told you.

                    DEBBIE
What else have you been lying about?

                    PETE
Nothing.

                    BEN
          (to Alison)
     That guy said, "Don't let the door hit
     you in the vagina on the way out."

                    DEBBIE
     Where were you on Wednesday?

                    PETE
     I'm going to be honest with you.

                    ALISON
          (to Ben)
     Yeah, I heard him.

                    BEN
          (to Alison)
     That was hilarious.

                    DEBBIE
     That would be a good idea.

                    PETE
     You've been mad because I've been working
     so much and I didn't want to upset you.

                    DEBBIE
     I wouldn't be mad.

                    PETE
     You would be.

                    DEBBIE
     I don't get mad.

                    PETE
     It's a fantasy baseball draft. I'm not
     cheating or anything.

                    DEBBIE
     No, this is worse.

                    PETE
     How is this worse?

                    DEBBIE
     This is you wanting to be with your
     friends more than your family.

                    PETE
     Look, the reason I make that up is
     because if I told you what I was really
     doing, you would just get mad. So, you
     think I'm seeing a band, I do my fantasy
     draft, and it's win/win.

                    DEBBIE
     Well, what did you do last Wednesday
     night when you said you went to see a
     band?

                    PETE
     I went to the movies.

                    DEBBIE
     With who?

                    PETE
By myself.

                    DEBBIE
What'd you see?

                    PETE
"Spiderman Three."

                    DEBBIE
Why do you want to go by yourself? Why
didn't you ask me to go?

                    PETE
Because I needed to get away, you know?
With work and you and the kids, sometimes
I just need some time to myself.

                    DEBBIE
I need time for myself. I want time for
myself, too.

Debbie holds back tears.

                    DEBBIE (cont'd)
You're not the only one.

                    PETE
It's not that big of a deal.

                    DEBBIE
        (through tears)
I like Spiderman.

                    PETE
Okay, so let's see "Spiderman Three" next
week.

                    DEBBIE
I don't want to go see it now.

                    PETE
Well...

                    DEBBIE
I don't want to have to ask you to ask
me. I want you to just come up with it on
your own.

                    PETE
What? I don't even know what to say. Uh,
what do you want me to do?

                    DEBBIE
You just think because you don't yell
that you're not mean, but this is mean.

                    PETE
I'm not being mean. I'm being honest.
You're telling me I need to be honest.
Just--

                    DEBBIE
No, you're not. You're lying.

                    PETE
          I'm doing it because I need to keep my
          sanity a little bit.

                    DEBBIE
          You know what? I don't want you at the
          house anymore. Okay?

                    PETE
          Come on.

Debbie heads for the car.

                    BEN
          Oh, shit, she's coming back.

I/E ALISON CAR - DAY

Alison drives to the gynecologist with Ben.

                    BEN
          How come we go to the gynecologist so
          often? I bet we have to go so much so we
          can pay for that three-hundred-thousand-
          dollar machine he has.

                    ALISON
          I cannot stop thinking about what an
          asshole Pete is.

                    BEN
          That's a little strong, I would say.

                    ALISON
          Really? Because that had to be one of the
          most selfish things I've ever witnessed.

                    BEN
          It's understandable. I even think it's
          kind of funny.

                    ALISON
          What's funny about it?

                    BEN
          Well, you won't laugh now, I wouldn't
          imagine, but you know, the situation. We
          break into this stranger's house thinking
          we're going to find him sleeping with a
          woman, and then it's a bunch of nerds
          playing fantasy baseball.If you saw that
          on television, you would laugh.

                    ALISON
          Is that what you think?

                    BEN
          Yeah.

                    ALISON
          Is that what you want to do, Ben?

                    BEN
I don't even like baseball. I'm just
saying when you're a guy and you have a
family and you have responsibility, you
lose that male camaraderie, and I get
that. I totally understand where he's
coming from.

                    ALISON
Why do you guys always go to that place?
You miss male camaraderie. What do I give
a shit? Go hang out with your bearded
freak friends. I don't care. You want to
hang out with guys that look like the
Shoe Bomber, it's all on you, man.

                    BEN
Well what the fuck am I supposed to say
to that?

                    ALISON
You should just support me! You know, you
should just support everything I say
because at this juncture in my life, I'm
allowed to be wrong!

                    BEN
So if you're wrong, I have to support it?

                    ALISON
Yes!

                    BEN
I can't tell you that you're acting like
a lunatic?

                    ALISON
Oh, that's helpful. You have to do
nothing!

                    BEN
I've sacrificed a lot of shit to this!

                    ALISON
You are just fucking sitting there! You
haven't sacrificed anything!

                    BEN
I have.

                    ALISON
I've had to sacrifice my job, my body, my
youth, my vagina!

                    BEN
You've sacrificed your vagina?

                    ALISON
Yes! It will never look the same after
this!

                    BEN
Well. Fine. I'll pay for vaginal
reconstructive surgery.

                    ALISON
You can't pay for shit! You can barely
buy spaghetti.

                    BEN
You're right. Fine!

                    ALISON
You know what? Get out of the car.

                    BEN
Oh! You know what? Why don't you not
threaten me?!

                    ALISON
You should just get out of the fucking
car.

                    BEN
I'm not going to get out of the car in
the middle of nowhere! No!

                    ALISON
Get out of the car.

                    BEN
No!

                    ALISON
I own this car! Get out of my car!

                    BEN
No.

                    ALISON
Get out of my car!

                    BEN
No.

                    ALISON
     (yelling)
Get out of my fucking car!

Ben gets out of the car and immediately KNOCKS on the window.

                    BEN
Can you let me back in the car, please?
Have you calmed down? Did you take a
breath? I have no clue where we are!

Alison just glares at him.

                    BEN (cont'd)
Fine. Go. Great.

Alison drives off.

INT. DR. HOWARD'S OFFICE - LATER

Alison stands on a scale while DR. HOWARD'S NURSE weighs her.

                    ALISON
You know what? Maybe I should take my
shoes off. Or my belt buckle. My belt
buckle's huge.

                    DR. HOWARD'S NURSE
          Don't worry about gaining weight. Your
          baby wants you to gain a whole mess of
          weight.

Ben walks into the room, winded.

                    ALISON
               (to Ben)
          Are you fucking kidding me?

                    BEN
          Why don't you take off your earrings,
          too? They weigh about eighty pounds.
          They're made out of moon rocks aren't
          they?

                    ALISON
          Do not make fun of me. Okay? I am
          hormonal, I am terrified, and I am
          falling apart, so stop treating
          everything like it's a big joke!

                    BEN
          I'm sorry you're freaking out, but I just
          walked three fucking miles through
          Koreatown to get here. Sorry if I'm
          trying to lighten the mood a little.

The Nurse leaves.

                    ALISON
          Well, don't! Okay?! You can't take
          anything seriously! You didn't even read
          the baby books.

                    BEN
          I didn't read the baby books! What's
          gonna happen? How did anyone ever give
          birth without a baby book?! That's right,
          the ancient Egyptians fucking engraved
          "What to Expect When You're Expecting" on
          the pyramid walls! I forgot about that!
          Who gives a flying fuck about the baby
          books?!

                    ALISON
          It just shows your lack of commitment,
          Ben! That you're not in this with me!

                    BEN
          Did you just say my lack of commitment?
          Because that's what it sounded like. It
          almost seems as though you forgot I
          proposed to you like an asshole! And you
          said no to me!

                    ALISON
          If you feel that way, you should just go.
          Really. Just go. Because we didn't mean
          to do this together, okay? And, and we
          tried to make it work and that was good,
          I suppose.

Alison holds back tears.

                    ALISON (cont'd)
But it doesn't work. Because we are two
completely different people. And I think
it would just be easier for both of us if
we stop fooling ourselves.

                    BEN
You know what? I know this isn't you
talking, it's your hormones, but I would
just like to say, "Fuck you, hormones!
You are a crazy bitch, hormones! Not
Alison! Hormones!" Fuck them. It's a
girl. Buy some pink shit!

                    ALISON
Nice. You are such an asshole. You know
what? Go fuck your fucking bong, you
fuck!

                    BEN
I will fuck my bong. Doggie-style, for
once.

Ben exits while giving Alison the finger as her walks away.
Dr. Howard's Nurse returns.

                    DR. HOWARD'S NURSE
Are you ready?

                    ALISON
I'm really sorry about all that. That was
really inappropriate.

                    DR. HOWARD'S NURSE
That's okay. It happens all the time
here. It's fine.

                    ALISON
I don't feel so stupid, then.

                    DR. HOWARD'S NURSE
Not at all.

EXT. DEL'S SALOON - NIGHT

Establishing shot.

INT. DEL'S SALOON

Ben and Pete drink at the bar.

                    BEN
I totally know what you're talking about,
man. If I wrote out the list of shit
Alison doesn't let me do it would be
endless. Don't smoke pot. Don't have
samurai swords in your room. Don't have
illegal grow operations in the house. I
could go on all fucking day. Have I told
her to stop doing anything ever? No.

                    PETE
Marriage is like that show "Everybody
Loves Raymond," but it's not funny. All
the problems are the same, but it's...
                         (MORE)

                    PETE (cont'd)
Instead of all the funny, pithy dialogue,
everybody's just really pissed off and
tense. Marriage is like an unfunny, tense
version of "Everybody Loves Raymond," but
it doesn't last twenty-two minutes. It
lasts forever.

                    BEN
Let's get out of here, man. Honestly,
let's just go. Let's go to Vegas.

                    PETE
Let's do it.

                    BEN
Yeah.

                    PETE
Why not?

INT. ALISON'S HOUSE - NIGHT

Alison watches a pregnancy show on TV. Debbie marches into
the guest house.

                    DEBBIE
Get up.

                    ALISON
What?

                    DEBBIE
We're not going to do this. Seriously.

Debbie turns off the television.

                    ALISON
What are you doing?

                    DEBBIE
We have to do something! And have fun!

                    ALISON
I'm just so tired.

                    DEBBIE
I know you're tired. But we're going to
be untired! We're going to go live!

                    ALISON
Ugh. I hate you so much sometimes.

                    DEBBIE
We're going to be positive.

                    ALISON
How many Red Bulls have you had?

                    DEBBIE
I've had about three Red Bulls in the
last fifteen minutes. And I feel
fabulous! We're going to create a new
life and it's going to be awesome! Let's
go!

EXT. BEN'S HOUSE

Ben and Pete KNOCK on the front door.

                    BEN
          Since when do we lock this fucking thing?
          Come on!

Jason opens the door with Jonah and Jay. All of their eyes
are very infected.

                    JASON
          Yo. We can't go, dude. Sorry.

                    BEN
          Holy crap! What happened?

                    JONAH
          We got pink eye.

                    BEN
          What? You giving each other butterfly
          kisses or something?

                    JASON
          Very funny. That's not how you get pink
          eye. You get it from poo particles making
          their way into your ocular cavities.

                    JAY
          Hey, Ben.

                    BEN
          Yo.

                    JAY
          How's it going? I farted on Jason's
          pillow as a practical joke. He farted on
          Jonah's, thinking it was mine. And then
          eventually pink-eyes my pillow. I'm not
          proud of this. But, I think we've all
          forgiven each other. But, we can't go
          anywhere.

                    PETE
          You can get pink eye from farting in a
          pillow?

                    JONAH
          Totally.

                    PETE
          That's awesome.

                    JONAH
          Yeah, but you got to be bare-assed.

Martin enters the doorway, his eyes are the worst.

                    BEN
          Jesus. Martin got it bad! What, did
          someone take a dump right in your eye?

                    MARTIN
          No. No pink eye for me. I'm just
          really...high.

                    BEN
          Well stay back, guys. I got to get my
          suit.

Ben enters the house and the guys pretend they're going to
rub their faces on him. Pete stays outside.

                    JASON
               (to Pete)
          Are you Debbie's husband?

                    PETE
          Yeah.

Jason shuts the door on Pete.

I/E. PETE'S CONVERTIBLE - NIGHT

Pete drives with Ben to Vegas. They are wearing suits.

                    BEN
          This is fun!

                    PETE
          This is great. We're going to have the
          best time ever.

                    BEN
          We make a good team, man.

                    PETE
          Yep. It's like I can't come here with
          Debbie. She doesn't understand. It's like
          she wants to hold me in, and she was
          telling Alison she could train you.

                    BEN
          She thinks she could train me?

                    PETE
          Yeah, like you're running the Triple
          Crown.

                    BEN
          She can't train this! I'm like Siegfried
          and Roy's Bengal. You think I'm trained.
          I'll bite your fucking face off.

                    PETE
          That's right.

                    BEN
          In front of a crowd, baby.

                    PETE
          This is better. Besides I don't know if I
          have enough of these babies to go around.

Pete brandishes a bag of mushrooms.

                    BEN
          Oh, my God. Are these mushrooms?

                    PETE
          I got them from a roadie for the Black
          Crowes.

                    BEN
          I'm eating them.

                    PETE
          Oh, no, save it! I got tickets to Cirque
          du Soleil.

                    BEN
          You do?! No you don't.

                    PETE
          I swear to God, man.

                    BEN
          Holy shit!

                    PETE
          I see the beam of light.

                    BEN
          There it is, baby.

                    PETE
          Woo-hoo. You're so money that you don't
          even know how much money you have.

INT. STRIP CLUB

Ben and Pete receive lap dances from topless strippers.

                    BEN
          I love Vegas, man.

                    PETE
          This is the greatest place on earth.

                    BEN
          It's really amazing here.

The stripper straddles Pete and pulls his tie through her
legs so that he face is pulled against her butt.

                    PETE
          Whoa. You got my tie. This is awesome.

                    BEN
          Now that's how you get pink eye.

EXT. NIGHTCLUB - NIGHT

Debbie and Alison approach the nightclub, passing the line,
straight to the DOORMAN. The Doorman lets TWO PRETTY GIRLS
past the rope.

                    DOORMAN
               (to the Two Pretty Girls)
          Hey, what's up, baby girl?

Debbie and Alison move up to the doorman.

                    DEBBIE
          Hi.

                    DOORMAN
          What's up? End of the line, please.

                    DEBBIE
Really?

                    DOORMAN
Yeah.

                    DEBBIE
Oh, come on.

                    DOORMAN
Look, we're at capacity, okay? We'll let
some people in when it clears out a
little. You'll get right in if you go
back to the end of the line.

                    DEBBIE
We come here all the time. It's not a big
deal. It doesn't really look that crowded
in there.

                    DOORMAN
Hey, look, I don't make the rules.

                    DEBBIE
Please?

                    DOORMAN
No.

TWO CUTE GIRLS approach. The Doorman lifts the rope for them.

                    DOORMAN (cont'd)
Hey, what's up, shorty? What's up pretty
girls? See y'all when y'all get out. Take
care of yourself.

                    DEBBIE
What was that? What the fuck was that?

                    DOORMAN
It is what it is, sweetie. Now can you
step to the back, please?

                    ALISON
     (to Debbie)
You know what? Maybe we should just go.

                    DEBBIE
You don't need to call me sweetie.

                    DOORMAN
Yeah, but maybe you should listen to your
friend.

                    DEBBIE
No, you don't need to call me sweetie.

                    DOORMAN
All right, you want to come in, you're
going to have to go to the end of the
line and wait like everybody else.

                    DEBBIE
I'm not going to go to the end of the
fucking line. Who the fuck are you? I
have just as much of a right to be here
as any of these little skanky girls!
                    (MORE)

Alison Scott (KATHERINE HEIGL) and Ben Stone (SETH ROGEN)

All photos by Suzanne Hanover

SETH ROGEN as
Ben Stone

KATHERINE HEIGL as
Alison Scott

LESLIE MANN as Alison's sister, Debbie

PAUL RUDD as Alison's brother-in-law, Pete

Alison's nieces, Sadie (MAUDE APATOW, left) and Charlotte (IRIS APATOW)

Left to right: Martin (MARTIN STARR), Ben (SETH ROGEN), Jason (JASON SEGEL), Jonah (JONAH HILL), and Jay (JAY BARUCHEL)

JONAH HILL as Jonah

JAY BARUCHEL as Jay

JASON SEGEL as Jason

MARTIN STARR as Martin

Left to right: Jodi (CHARLYNE YI), Martin (MARTIN STARR), Jonah
(JONAH HILL), and Ben (SETH ROGEN)

Alison (KATHERINE HEIGL) ready to celebrate her promotion.

Alison (KATHERINE HEIGL) and her sister, Debbie (LESLIE MANN), take a number of pregnancy tests.

Alison (KATHERINE HEIGL) and Ben (SETH ROGEN) share a meal.

Alison's family at breakfast—including nieces Sadie (MAUDE APATOW) and Charlotte (IRIS APATOW), sister Debbie (LESLIE MANN), and brother-in-law Pete (PAUL RUDD).

Alison's sister, Debbie (LESLIE MANN), and brother-in-law, Pete (PAUL RUDD).

Debbie (LESLIE MANN) and Alison (KATHERINE HEIGL) evaluate Ben's parenting skills.

Ben (SETH ROGEN) and Pete and Debbie's youngest daughter, Charlotte (IRIS APATOW), play house.

Alison (KATHERINE HEIGL) and Ben (SETH ROGEN) shop for baby gear.

Alison (KATHERINE HEIGL) and Ben (SETH ROGEN) at their first
OB/GYN appointment.

Alison (KATHERINE HEIGL) and Ben (SETH ROGEN) share a romantic moment.

Ben (SETH ROGEN) finally reading the baby books.

Ben (SETH ROGEN) and his dad (HAROLD RAMIS) have a man-to-man chat.

Pete (PAUL RUDD) and Ben (SETH ROGEN) commiserate over drinks.

Ben (SETH ROGEN) and Pete (PAUL RUDD) at a kid's birthday.

Alison (KATHERINE HEIGL), sister Debbie (LESLIE MANN), boyfriend Ben (SETH ROGEN), and brother-in-law Pete (PAUL RUDD) prepare for the baby's arrival.

KATHERINE HEIGL as Alison and LESLIE MANN as her sister Debbie on camera.

SETH ROGEN as Ben, JAY BARUCHEL as Jay, and writer/director/producer JUDD APATOW on the set.

Writer/director/producer JUDD APATOW on the set.

                    DEBBIE (cont'd)
What, am I not skanky enough for you?!
You want me to hike up my fucking skirt?!
What the fuck is your problem?! I'm not
going anywhere! You're just some 'roided
out freak with a fucking clipboard. And
your stupid little fucking rope! You may
have power now, but you're not God.
You're a doorman! Okay? You're a doorman!
So...fuck you, you fucking fag with your
fucking little faggy gloves.

The Doorman grabs Debbie and takes her aside.

                    DOORMAN
Come here, come on.

The Doorman takes Debbie aside.

                    DOORMAN
          (whispering)
I know. You're right. I'm so sorry. I
fucking hate this job. I don't want to be
the one to pass judgement and decide who
gets in. This shit makes me sick to my
stomach. I get the runs from the stress.
It's not because you're not hot. I would
love to tap that ass. I would tear that
ass up. I can't let you in because you're
old as fuck...for this club, not, you
know, for the earth.

                    DEBBIE
What?

                    DOORMAN
You old. She pregnant. Can't have a bunch
of old, pregnant bitches running around.
That's crazy. I'm only allowed to let in
five percent black people. He said that.
Five percent. That mean if there's twenty-
five people here, I get to let in one-and-
a-quarter black people. So I got to hope
there's a black midget in the crowd.

                    DEBBIE
Now I feel guilty. I'm sorry.

                    DOORMAN
Why y'all want to be in here anyway?
Y'all need to be at a yoga class or
something.

          (regarding Alison)
What the fuck is she doing at the club?
That's not even good parenting right
there. Your old ass should know better
than that.

                    DEBBIE
Oh, God. Ugh.

Debbie takes Alison away.

EXT. VEGAS POOL - NIGHT

Ben and Pete hold neon yard glasses and walk past numerous
swimsuit-clad men and women.

                         BEN
              Have the mushrooms kicked in yet?

Ben and Pete CHUCKLE uncontrollably.

EXT. TREASURE ISLAND HOTEL - NIGHT

Establishing shot.

INT. CIRQUE DU SOLEIL

Ben and Pete watch from the crowd as acrobats climb poles.

                    BEN AND PETE
              Ohhhhhh!

                         BEN
              This was a great idea, man.

                         PETE
              This is the best idea I've ever had in my
              life.

Two bare-chested male acrobats start to balance on top of
each other.

                         BEN
              What are they going to do? What in the
              world are they doing? If I shaved my
              stomach and my chest, I would look
              exactly like that. Those guys are at work
              right now.
                    (imitating one of the acrobats)
              What'd you do today? Oh, just lifted my
              brother.

The crowd starts to APPLAUD for the acrobats.

                    BEN (cont'd)
              No! Don't applaud! He'll fall! I'm
              freaking out right now, man!

Many acrobats in devilish outfits take the stage.

                    BEN (cont'd)
              The mushrooms are turning on me!

A clown dressed as a GIANT BABY is part of the act. Ben YELLS
frantically.

                    GIANT BABY
              Papa.

                         BEN
              I am not your papa.

A giant Snail comes out onto the stage.

                    BEN (cont'd)
              I can't deal with this shit, man!

Ben stands up and runs down the aisle towards the exit.

EXT. STREET NEAR NIGHTCLUB - NIGHT

Debbie and Alison sit on the curb.

> DEBBIE
> (weeping)
> It's over.

> ALISON
> What's over?

> DEBBIE
> My youth.

> ALISON
> Don't say that.

> DEBBIE
> It's true. I just want to dance. I love
> dancing.

> ALISON
> So dance.

> DEBBIE
> I can't dance. I'm embarrassed.

> ALISON
> I should be embarrassed. I'm a fucking
> whale and I'm trying to get into some
> stupid club and--

> DEBBIE
> You look beautiful. You're young and
> you're tall and you got the good lips and
> boobs. I'm going to be alone.

> ALISON
> Debbie, no, you're not.

> DEBBIE
> Yes, I am. Oh, God! Fucking, men! I get
> worse looking and he gets better looking,
> and it's so fucking unfair. Oh, fuck. We
> should go. My babysitter always gets mad
> when we come home past twelve. She's such
> a pissy little high-school cunt.

INT. VEGAS HOTEL ROOM - NIGHT

Ben curls up on the bed with his shirt and boxers on. A scene
from "CHEAPER BY THE DOZEN" plays on the television. Steve
Martin juggles all of his children.

> STEVE MARTIN
> (on TV)
> Let's move, gang! Come on, come on, come
> on! Jessica, can you get these plates and
> put them on the table, please?!

> BEN
> This isn't funny. That guy has twelve
> kids. It's not funny. This is sick. This
> is a sick movie. That's a lot of
> responsibility to be joking about. That's
> not funny. I got to turn this off. It's
> freaking me out.

Pete moves several chairs into the bedroom.

                    PETE
          There are five different types of chairs
          in this hotel room.

                    BEN
          Holy fuck. What are they all doing in
          here?

                    PETE
          These are five different types of chair.

                    BEN
          Get them out of here, man. This is too
          many chairs for one room.

                    PETE
          There's a guy that works for this hotel.
          His whole job is to find chairs.

Pete moves to a tall chair.

                    PETE (cont'd)
          Look at this one. Look at it. It's gold
          and red and it's kind of shiny. Shiny
          thread? Unbelievable. It is beautiful,
          and it feels amazing.

                    BEN
          The tall one's gawking at me and the
          short one's being very droll. I don't
          like them.

Pete switches to another chair.

                    PETE
          Oh, wow!

                    BEN
          It's weird that chairs even exist when
          you're not sitting on them.

Pete switched to another tall chair.

                    PETE
          I'm up high! I'm really high up.

                    BEN
          I should've read the baby books.

                    PETE
          Why didn't you read the baby books?

                    BEN
          Because then it's real, you know?

                    PETE
          Dude, it's real whether or not you read
          those books. That baby's coming.

Pete sits on another chair.

                    PETE (cont'd)
          Oh, man!

                         BEN
          Think they'll take us back?

                         PETE
          Yes. But I don't know why. Do you ever
          wonder how somebody could even like you?

                         BEN
          All the time, man. Like every day. I
          wonder how you like me.

                         PETE
          How can Debbie like me? She likes me. I
          mean, she loves me. The biggest problem
          in our marriage is that she wants me
          around. She loves me so much that she
          wants me around all the time. That's our
          biggest problem. And I can't even accept
          that? Uh, like that upsets me?!

Ben sits up from the bed.

                         BEN
          What?

                         PETE
          She's the one. She loves me.

                         BEN
          You can't believe...that people love you?
          I love you, man! Debbie loves you!

                         PETE
          I don't think I can accept her love.
          There's something wrong with me.

                         BEN
          You can't accept love?

                         PETE
          I don't know what it is.

                         BEN
          Love? The most beautiful, shiny, warmy
          thing in the world? You can't accept it?

                         PETE
          I have to go to this other chair.

Pete switches to a new chair.

                         PETE (cont'd)
          Oh, this is a better energy.

                         BEN
          You can't accept pure love? You can't
          accept Debbie? She's chosen to give you
          her life. She's picked you as her life
          partner! But you play fantasy baseball
          because you can't accept her love?

Ben BURPS.

                         BEN (cont'd)
          Ugh. I could accept it, man. And Debbie's
          amazing, man.
                         (MORE)

                              BEN (cont'd)
         She's cool and she's funny and she smells
         good and she's nice and her hair always
         looks different. She's too good for you,
         man.

Pete shoves his hand in his mouth.

                              PETE
         Tastes like a rainbow.

                              BEN
         You're disgusting. You're an urchin. And
         she busts your balls because you're a
         little bitch! You're a filthy bitch! And
         I'd bust your balls! Debbie wants to give
         her life to you and Alison doesn't want
         to do that with me. And it makes me sad
         all day. I want to go home.

                              PETE
                    (with fist in mouth)
         I want to go home, too.

EXT. DEBBIE AND PETE'S HOUSE - DAY

Establishing shot.

EXT. DEBBIE AND PETE'S HOUSE, BACKYARD

Debbie and Alison set up Sadie's princess birthday party.

                              ALISON
         Everything looks beautiful.

                              DEBBIE
         Thanks. I went kind of overboard, huh?

                              ALISON
         No, it's great.

                              DEBBIE
         Your daughter only turns eight once. Is
         Ben going to come?

                              ALISON
         I don't think so. I don't know why he
         would.

EXT. DEBBIE AND PETE'S HOUSE

Ben approaches the house with a present. He wears a button-
down shirt and long khaki shorts. He KNOCKS on the door.
Sadie opens the door.

                              BEN
         Oh, hey, what up dog?

                              SADIE
         Where have you been?

                              BEN
         Around. You know, just kind of doing my
         thing.

                              SADIE
         Why is everybody so mad at you?

             BEN
I don't know. Are they mad? What have
they been saying?

           SADIE
They've been saying, like "blah-blah-blah-
blah. Ben's a prick."

             BEN
They said that?

           SADIE
A lot.

             BEN
That sucks.

           SADIE
What does it mean?

             BEN
Penis. It means penis.

           SADIE
Oh.

   (chuckling)
Penis.

INT. DEBBIE AND PETE'S HOUSE, KITCHEN

Pete and Debbie prepare food as Ben walks in. Pete wears a
crown.

           PETE
Babe, we're running low on plates.
   (to Ben)
Hey Ben! What's up, man?

             BEN
What's happening, man?

          DEBBIE
Hey, Ben.

             BEN
Hey, Debbie.

          DEBBIE
How are you?

             BEN
Good. How are you?

Ben and Debbie kiss hello.

          DEBBIE
Hi.

   (to Pete)
Did you just get pink cupcakes or yellow
and pink cupcakes?

           PETE
I just got yellow cupcakes.

                    DEBBIE
          I thought I said to get pink cupcakes.

                    PETE
          I can run out. I'll get some more.

                    DEBBIE
          Nah, it's no big deal.

                    PETE
          I don't mind.

                    DEBBIE
          No it doesn't matter.

                    PETE
          You sure?

                    DEBBIE
          Yeah. You look really cute in that.

Pete and Debbie kiss. Debbie exits.

                    BEN
          Well, that was fast, you pussy.

                    PETE
          You're the one that got dressed up like a
          cholo on Easter to come to this party.

                    BEN
          How are things at Butt-Fucking-Ham
          Palace?

                    PETE
          You look like Babe Ruth's gay brother,
          Gabe Ruth.

                    BEN
          Well played, sir. That was good.

                    PETE
          You going to talk to Alison?

                    BEN
          Yeah, I was about to.

                    PETE
          Right on.

Ben hands Pete his gift for Sadie.

                    BEN
          It's a doll.

                    PETE
          Thanks, Ben.

EXT. DEBBIE AND PETE'S HOUSE, BACKYARD

Alison and Ben talk off to the side.

                    ALISON
          I just don't think we can make it work.

                    BEN
We can get back on track and everything's
going to be great.

                    ALISON
You're just being nice. And I'm being
nice and just because we're two nice
people doesn't mean we should stay
together. I don't want this baby to
determine the rest of our lives. You
know? Me not wanting to do this alone
isn't enough of a reason to drag you into
a relationship with me. It's just not
fair. And, and don't repeat this, but,
God, I don't want to end up like Debbie.

                    BEN
But Debbie's happy.

                    ALISON
She's happy today. But every day is a
constant struggle for them because
they're not right for each other. You
know? And they have to force it and I
don't want us to have to do that. I don't
want to force you to be what I think you
should be. That's wrong of me because
you're great. You really are. You're
great the way you are and, I mean, you
like to get high and you like to do
shrooms in Vegas.

                    BEN
I didn't do shrooms in Vegas.

                    ALISON
And who am I to stop you? Who am I to
tell you that that's wrong? It's not
wrong. It's who you are. It's what you
enjoy and that's your life and...

                    BEN
I'm not that guy anymore.

                    ALISON
We can be friends. And you can be there
when the baby is born, and in the baby's
life as much as you want. I hope you will
be.

                    BEN
If you give me a shot to just show you
that I'm con--

Debbie approaches.

                    DEBBIE
Excuse me?

                    BEN
Oh, shit.

                    DEBBIE
        (to Alison)
Can you grab the video camera? We're
going to sing "Happy Birthday" now.

>   ALISON
> Yeah.
>
>   (to Ben)
> I'm sorry. I got to go. I'm sorry.
>
>   BEN
> It's okay.
>
>   ALISON
> I'll be right back. We'll finish talking.

INT. DEBBIE AND PETE'S HOUSE, KITCHEN

Ben stomps back into the kitchen. Pete is carrying the
birthday cake.

>   PETE
> What happened?
>
>   BEN
> Thanks for warning me, man. I just
> walking into a fucking buzz saw! She
> rejected me! Because you, for some insane
> reason, told Debbie that I did mushrooms
> with you in Vegas! She gets mad because I
> smoke pot! Now I'm upping it to fucking
> psychedelics! Thanks!
>
>   PETE
> Really? I thought that she'd take you
> back.
>
>   BEN
> You know why she just rejected me?
> Because you're such a shitty husband, she
> thinks I'm going to turn into a shitty
> husband!

Ben exits. Pete starts to carry the cake to the backyard.

>   PETE
>   (singing)
> "Happy Birthday to you. Happy Birthday to
> you."

EXT. MTV MOVIE AWARDS - DAY

Alison interviews JESSICA ALBA.

>   JESSICA ALBA
> When are you due?
>
>   ALISON
> I got two months.
>
>   JESSICA ALBA
> Really? Wow. Well, you're so big already.
>
>   ALISON
> Yeah.

Alison interviews ANDY DICK.

>   ANDY DICK
> When is that baby popping out?

                    ALISON
          I got two months to go.

                    ANDY DICK
          Really? Are you dilated yet?

Andy tries to stick his hand up Alison's dress.

                    ALISON
          Wow, wow.

Alison interviews EVA MENDES.

                    EVA MENDES
          You look fantastic.

                    ALISON
          Thanks, thanks.

                    EVA MENDES
          Are you going to, like, give birth right
          now?

Alison interviews STEVE CARELL.

                    STEVE CARELL
          Wow! You're about to drop any second.

                    ALISON
          You know what?

                    STEVE CARELL
          I love your broach here.

                    ALISON
          You don't need to lie to me. I don't
          appreciate it. I know I look like a fat
          cow. And I'm sweating profusely.

                    STEVE CARELL
          No, you don't look like a...fat cow at
          all. You look great. So, I have to get
          going in. They're calling me.

                    ALISON
          Steve, hey! Help me out. Give me an
          interview, please.

                    STEVE CARELL
          Well, I just need to run in.

Steve starts to pull away.

                    ALISON
          You know what? Just say into the camera,
          "You're watching E! Entertainment." Just
          give me that.

                    STEVE CARELL
          Congratulations.

                    ALISON
          No, Steve, don't be an asshole! Come on.

                    STEVE CARELL
          I'm not being an asshole.

INT. EDITING BAY

Alison and Brent watch the MTV Movies Awards footage.

                    BRENT
          Wow. You managed to turn Steve Carell
          into an asshole. No easy feat.

               ALISON
          Shut up, Brent.

INT. BEN'S HOUSE - NIGHT

Ben sits on the couch and talks to Harris on the telephone.

                    BEN
          You screwed me, Dad, okay? You said
          everything was going to be fine and
          nothing is fine. Nothing is fine.

                    HARRIS (O.S.)
          Ben, I've been divorced three times. Why
          would you listen to me?

                    BEN
          Because you were the only one giving me
          advice! And it was, it was terrible
          advice!

                    HARRIS (O.S.)
          You can go around blaming everyone else,
          but in the end, until you take
          responsibility for yourself, none of this
          is going to work out.

                    BEN
          I don't know how to take responsibility
          for myself, okay? I didn't read the baby
          books!

                    HARRIS (O.S.)
          You didn't read the books?

                    BEN
          I should smoke less pot. I don't know
          what to do! I'm an idiot! What, tell me
          what to do!

                    HARRIS (O.S.)
          I don't know. I don't know. Ben, I love
          ya. What can I tell ya?

                    BEN
          Just tell me what to do.

INT. JETSET STUDIOS - DAY

Ben sits at his work desk as his new BOSS walks by. Ben has
gotten a job designing web pages.

                    BOSS
          Stone, you settling in okay?

                    BEN
          Best job I ever had.

                         BOSS
             Like to hear it.

INT. BEN'S NEW APARTMENT - DAY

Ben is being shown an apartment by a realtor.

INT. DR. HOWARD'S OFFICE

Dr. Howard gives Alison a sonogram. Ben is not there.

EXT. BEN'S HOUSE - DAY

Ben's roommates help him move his stuff into a moving van.

INT. YOGA STUDIO - DAY

Alison and Debbie participate in a baby exercise class among
other couples.

INT. BABY CLOTHES STORE

Ben asks a salesman about baby clothes.

INT. ALISON'S GUEST HOUSE - DAY

Alison folds baby clothes in her nursery.

INT. BEN'S NEW APARTMENT - DAY

Ben hangs up wrapping paper as wall paper in his makeshift
nursery.

INT. JACK'S OFFICE, E! ENTERTAINMENT - DAY

Alison, Jill and Jack are in the office.

                         JACK
             Alison, thank you for coming in. I don't
             want to shock you, but know what's under
             that jacket. You're pregnant, have been
             for a while. From my count, you're right
             around eight months. And I don't know why
             you felt you couldn't tell us.

                         ALISON
             I'm really sorry.

                         JILL
             This is Hollywood. We don't like liars.

                         ALISON
             I just wasn't expecting this and, I
             didn't know how to handle it, and I
             didn't want to lose my job. I'm really
             sorry.

                         JACK
             It's unfortunate that you didn't tell us
             because you would've found out that we
             thought it's great.

                         ALISON
             Really?

                    JILL
Yeah.

                    JACK
So, we did some research. And turns out,
people like pregnant.

                    ALISON
Oh, my God!

                    JACK
The bigger you are, the bigger your
numbers.

                    JILL
I was surprised because I feel the
opposite.

                    JACK
We're going to do a whole maternity month
on "E, Exclamation, Mommy." You're going
to interview all the pregnant celebs.

                    ALISON
Really?

                    JACK
Yes.

                    JILL
Scary!

                    JACK
If you're pregnant, they're pregnant, you
can talk about being pregnant.

                    JILL
It just grosses me out...when I know that
people are pregnant. Because I think
about the birth. Everything's so wet.

                    JACK
And everything that goes into it. None of
the gross stuff. But you know, hopes,
dreams, whatever. It's going to be great.

                    ALISON
Oh, my God. This is such good news. Thank
you so much.

                    JACK
You're welcome. And then, after the baby
is out, tighten it back up.

                    JILL
Tight. And please don't lie to us again.
Because maybe someday we could be
friends.

                    ALISON
Okay. I won't. I'm sorry.

                    JILL
I just don't like secrets.

INT. DEBBIE AND PETE'S HOUSE - DAY

Alison holds the door while Pete, Debbie, Charlotte and Sadie move their bags to the car.

                    PETE
          You know, it's a rare thing that you live
          to see the day your wildest dreams come
          true. I mean what is there left to want?
          I get to go to Legoland.

                    DEBBIE
          Shut up, Pete.

                    PETE
          Say it!

                    ALISON
          Legoland!

                    DEBBIE
          Don't get them all riled up before the
          drive.

                    PETE
          I shouldn't have given them all that meth
          then.

                    DEBBIE
          We'll be back on Sunday.

                    PETE
          Or Saturday. You never know. We might see
          it all in one day.

                    DEBBIE
          Sunday. Let's go.

INT. ALISON'S GUEST HOUSE - NIGHT

Alison watches the lesbian pool scene from "Wild Things." She suddenly gets a pain in her belly. She winces.

                    ALISON
          Ow, ow, ow.

INT. BEN'S NEW APARTMENT

Ben's phone RINGS.

                    BEN
          Hello?

INT. BEN'S OLD HOUSE - CONTINUOUS

Jason sits in a chair. Jonah stands behind him.

                    JASON
          Hey, what's up daddy? What are you doing?

INT. BEN'S NEW APARTMENT - CONTINUOUS

Ben reads a baby book.

                    BEN
          Just smoking a joint, drinking some
          beers, you know. Rocking.

INTERCUT:

                    JASON
          I think we're about to go to a new club.
          You coming?

                    BEN
          No. I'm going to pack it in soon.

                    JONAH
            (to Jason)
          What's he doing?

                    JASON
            (to Jonah)
          He says he's going to call it a night.
            (to Ben)
          Dude, it's like eight-fifteen, man.

                    BEN
          I know. I'm just tired.

                    JONAH
            (to Jason)
          Is he depressed?

                    JASON
            (to Ben)
          You depressed?

                    BEN
          No, I feel great. I like it.

                    JASON
            (to Jonah)
          He says no.

                    JONAH
            (to Jason)
          Ask him if he's going to kill himself.

                    JASON
            (to Ben)
          You going to kill yourself?

                    BEN
          No, I'm not. Okay? Thank you.

                    JONAH
            (to Jason)
          Tell him not to jerk off with a noose
          around his neck. It's dangerous.

                    JASON
            (to Ben)
          You shouldn't jerk off with a noose
          around your neck because it's dangerous.

                    BEN
          Okay, very good.

                         JONAH
                    (to Jason)
          Oh, and tell him if he has to, tell him
          he needs a teammate or a spotter there.

                         JASON
                    (to Ben)
          Right. And if you do, um, you should have
          a teammate or a spotter there.

                         BEN
          Great.

                         JASON
                    (to Jonah)
          He says your mom's already there.

                         JONAH
          That's cool, man.

INT. ALISON'S GUEST HOUSE

Alison paces while on the phone.

                         ALISON
                    (to herself)
          Okay, okay, okay.

                    (into the phone)
          Hi, Dr. Howard?

INT. MEXICAN RESTARAUNT - CONTINUOUS

DR. ANGELO walks into the restaraunt.

                         DR. ANGELO
          No, this is Dr. Angelo. How can I help
          you?

INT. ALISON'S GUEST HOUSE - CONTINUOUS

                         ALISON
          I'm a patient of Dr. Howard's and I'm
          going into labor and I need to speak with
          him.

INTERCUT:

                         DR. ANGELO
          I actually don't know where he is
          tonight. But I've made myself available
          to his patients and I'd be happy to help
          you.

                         ALISON
          Can you help me find him? Can you give me
          his number?

                         DR. ANGELO
          Oh, no. You know what? Actually, I'm
          under strict instructions not give out
          his number, but I can help you through
          this.

                         ALISON
          No, no, no, no. I want to speak to my own
          doctor.
                    (MORE)

                    ALISON (cont'd)
        You really won't give me his number?
        Because this is my first baby and he
        promised that he would be here for me and
        I need you to give me his number, okay?

                    DR. ANGELO
        Dr. Howard is not available tonight. Bet
        everything's going to be okay, I assure
        you.

                    ALISON
        No, I don't want you to help me because I
        have no idea who you are! I want my own
        goddamned doctor! You make sure he calls
        me!

Alison clicks off the phone.

                    ALISON (cont'd)
            (to herself)
        Oh, shit. Okay. Oh, shit.

Alison calls Ben.

INT. BEN'S NEW APARTMENT

Ben's sleeps in his bed. His phone RINGS. He blindly fishes
for the phone.

                    BEN
        Hello?

I/E BEN'S CAR - NIGHT

Ben feverishly drives to Alison.

                    BEN
            (to car)
        Oh, don't run out of gas! Don't run out
        of gas! Come on!

INT. ALISON'S GUEST HOUSE - NIGHT

Ben runs into Alison's guest house. It is empty.

                    BEN
        Hello?

EXT. DEBBIE AND PETE'S HOUSE, BACKYARD

Ben uses the back door to get into the house.

INT. DEBBIE AND PETE'S HOUSE, BEDROOM

Ben checks every room in the house.

                    BEN
        Please be in here. Hello? Hello!

INT. DEBBIE AND PETE'S HOUSE, BATHROOM

Ben finds Alison in a bubble bath surrounded by candles and
SOOTHING MUSIC.

                    BEN
        Hello? Alison. Hello?

> ALISON
> Ben?

> BEN
> Alison. What is this, like a water birth? What are we doing? Should we go?

> ALISON
> Shh! Just relax, okay? Just be mellow, because that's what this is all about. Because if it gets too stressful in here then the baby is born into a stressful environment and then he's wired for stress for the rest of his life. So just...just be calm.

> BEN
> (whispering)
> Okay. Okay. Let's relax. Do you want to talk about things? I feel really bad about a lot of the shit I did. I can't believe I said some of that. That's all I think about in my head. It--

> ALISON
> I don't want to talk about it.

> BEN
> But maybe we could bring the baby into a reconciled place so, we can talk--

> ALISON
> No. I don't want to go there. Don't go there, okay?

> BEN
> Okay.

> ALISON
> Help me stay relaxed.

> BEN
> So, what should I do?

> ALISON
> You need to call Dr. Howard.

Ben goes into the hall and calls Dr. Howard's house.

INT. DR. HOWARD'S HOUSE

Dr. Howard's housekeeper, MARIA, answers the phone.

> MARIA
> Hello?

INT. DEBBIE AND PETE'S HOUSE, BATHROOM

> BEN
> Hello, this is Ben Stone. I'm calling on behalf of Alison Scott. We need Dr. Howard. It's an emergency.

INT. DR. HOWARD'S HOUSE

                    MARIA
          He's at San Francisco at Bar Mitzvah.

INTERCUT:

                    BEN
          He's at a Bar Mitzvah in San Francisco?
          Do you know when he gets back?

                    MARIA
          In three days.

                    BEN
          Do you have his cell number, by any
          chance?

Ben pops his head around the corner to talk to Alison.

                    BEN (cont'd)
               (to Alison)
          Hey! Good news. I got his number right
          here. I'm going to call him right now.

                    ALISON
          Great. Thank you so much. I'm so glad
          you're here. Thank you.

                    BEN
          I'm glad I'm here, too. Thank you. I
          shouldn't have told you you were a
          fucking lunatic. I shouldn't have said
          that. I feel terrible about it.

                    ALISON
          No, it's okay. We're past it. I'm sorry I
          told you to fuck your bong.

                    BEN
          It's okay. I didn't.

                    ALISON
          Let's just drop it now. We're over it.

                    BEN
          I'm going to call him right now. You're
          doing so great.

Ben slips into the hallway and calls Dr. Howard.

                    DR. HOWARD (O.S.)
          Hello, it's Dr. Howard. I'm not here
          right now. Please leave a message.

                    BEN
               (into the phone)
          Hey, Doc Howard. Ben Stone calling. Guess
          what the fuck's up? Alison's going into
          labor and you are not fucking here. Now,
          where are you? You're at a fucking Bar
          Mitzvah in San Francisco, you
          motherfucking piece of shit! And you know
          I'm going to have to do now? I'm going to
          have to kill you. I'm going to have to
          pop a cap in your ass. You're dead!
          You're Tupac!
                    (MORE)

                         BEN (cont'd)
          You are fucking Biggie, you piece of
          shit! I hope you fucking die or drop the
          fucking chair and kill that fucking kid!
          Hope your plane crashes. Peace, fucker!

Ben goes back to Alison.

                         ALISON
          Hey.

                         BEN
          Hey.

                         ALISON
          Did you talk to him?

                         BEN
          I didn't talk to him directly, I left him
          a very nice message, though. What I'm
          about to tell you isn't that bad. You
          should know that going in. We can get
          through this and it's just a little
          hiccup, but everything will be fine. Do
          you trust me when I say everything will
          be fine?

                         ALISON
          I can deal with it.

                         BEN
          Okay. So, Dr. Howard is at a Bar Mitzvah.

                         ALISON
          A Bar Mitzvah?

                         BEN
          It's a Jewish rite of passage. And he's
          going to be there for the next three
          days, so he will not be able to be here
          tonight.

                         ALISON
          It's okay. What do you think we should
          do?

                         BEN
          I know exactly what to do. All we do is
          we'll get in the car, I'll drive to the
          hospital, and on the way, we will call
          every gynecologist we've met. Someone
          will be available. You know?

                         ALISON
          I can do that.

                         BEN
          Good. We still have time. I mean, how far
          apart are your contractions?

                         ALISON
          I think, like, seven minutes.

                         BEN
          Seven minutes! See? Not until four
          minutes is it really coming. And has your
          water broken, even?

                    ALISON
          I don't know. I'm in the tub.

                    BEN
          That's a good point. Have you had, have
          you had your bloody show?

                    ALISON
          What's that?

                    BEN
          It's a bloody mucusy discharge. But it
          only comes out right before the baby's
          going to come, so if that hasn't
          happened, we have time. We can make it to
          the hospital. It's no problem.

                    ALISON
          You read the baby books.

                    BEN
          Yeah. I did. I read three of them,
          actually.

                    ALISON
          Thank you.

                    BEN
          You're welcome.

EXT. HOSPITAL - NIGHT

Ben drives Alison's car. They park in a handicapped spot.

                    ALISON
          Wait. Are we allowed to park here?

                    BEN
          It's okay.

Ben takes a handicapped placard out of his jacket pocket and
hangs it on the mirror.

                    BEN (cont'd)
          I stole this from Martin's grandma.

                    ALISON
          Oh. That was really sweet of you.

                    BEN
          Thanks.

INT. HOSPITAL - FRONT DESK

Alison and Ben approach the desk. A male nurse, SAMUEL, and a
FEMALE NURSE tend to them.

                    BEN
               (to Alison)
          We're close. Home stretch.

               (to Female Nurse)
          Hello. This is Alison Scott. Dr. Kuni
          said he would let you know we were
          coming?

                    FEMALE NURSE
He did. We'll take good care of you.
Samuel?

                    SAMUEL
Yeah?

                    FEMALE NURSE
This is Alison Scott. Please admit her
into room 307.

                    SAMUEL
All right. Hi.

                    BEN
You're our nurse?

                    SAMUEL
That's why I'm holding the clipboard. So,
uh, what else is up with you guys?

Ben and Alison stare at Samuel.

                    SAMUEL (cont'd)
I'm just joking. Let's have a baby!

INT. HOSPITAL ROOM

Samuel is adjusting Alison's IV.

                    SAMUEL
So, I'm sorry it took me so long to find
that vein. That little guy really didn't
want me to find him.

                    ALISON
Is that the baby on that one right there?

Alison points to some equipment by her bed side.

                    SAMUEL
Yeah. That's how we can tell how the
little guy or gal is doing.

                    ALISON
Okay.

A groggy Dr. Kuni enters.

                    DR. KUNI
Hello, Alison, Ben. Interesting night.

                    BEN
We really, really appreciate you coming,
man.

                    DR. KUNI
What else do I have to do, I mean,
besides sleep? I was only kidding. What
happened to your doctor?

                    BEN
He's at a Bar Mitzvah in San Francisco.
He didn't tell us though.

                    DR. KUNI
Nice.

                    BEN
Yeah.

                    DR. KUNI
Lucky for you I don't have any Jewish
friends.

                    ALISON
Dr. Kuni, I really want to do this
naturally. I don't want to use drugs.

                    DR. KUNI
Let's just take a look and see what
happens, okay? Fetal heart rate is good.
Samuel, where are we?

                    SAMUEL
Four centimeters.

                    DR. KUNI
Four centimeters what?

                    SAMUEL
Dilated.

                    DR. KUNI
Dilated. That's right. Focus. Pay
attention, okay? We're a team. Okay?

INT. HOSPITAL - WAITING ROOM

Jonah, Jason, Jay and Martin sit in the waiting room.

                    JONAH
I want to get the fuck out of here.

                    JAY
What?

                    JONAH
I just want to get the fuck out of here.

                    JAY
Just relax, man, just relax.

                    JONAH
I don't fucking like hospitals.

                    JAY
Jonah, this is beautiful. I just think
you need to relax and embrace the beauty
of another life joining our gang. We're
having a baby. We are having a baby.

                    JONAH
I'm not having shit besides a fucking
panic attack. There's probably a fucking
room back there full of dead bodies! You
guys want to be here when one rolls out
and just fucking coughs malaria into our
face?

                    JAY
          Jesus.

                    JONAH
          Fucking shit.

INT. HOSPITAL ROOM

Ben massages Alison's back.

                    BEN
          Is that good?

                    ALISON
          Oh, yeah, get in there.

                    BEN
          I could do this all day.

The fetal heart monitors begins to BEEP.

                    ALISON
          What was that?

                    BEN
          What the hell was that?

Samuel hurries in to check the monitor.

                    BEN (cont'd)
          What's that, what's happening?

Dr. Kuni enters.

                    DR. KUNI
          Well, boy and girls, what seems to be the
          problem?

                    SAMUEL
          Decels.

                    DR. KUNI
          Oh, dear. Okay. Alison, I need you to
          turn on your back now, okay? The baby's
          heart rate is slowing. Okay?

                    BEN
          It's going to be okay.

               (to Dr. Kuni)
          Is it going to be fine?

Alison turns onto her back.

                    DR. KUNI
          It's going to be fine. Okay?

               (to Alison)
          You're going to feel a little bit of a
          push.

Dr. Kuni tries to reposition the baby.

                    BEN
          What are you doing?

                    DR. KUNI
          I'm turning the baby so I can take the
          pressure off the cord.

                    ALISON
          Oh, my God.

The monitors stops beeping.

                    DR. KUNI
          We're good. The heartbeat's stronger, but
          we're not out of the woods. We need to
          get things going now. I think the cord is
          wrapped around the neck. Okay?

                    BEN
          What?

                    DR. KUNI
          So I'm going to give you some medicine,
          pop the bag and get things going, okay? I
          don't want to leave the baby in there for
          long and we can give you some medicine
          for the pain.

                    ALISON
          No, no, no, no. I don't want the baby to
          be born all drugged out. It's not my
          birth plan.

                    DR. KUNI
          Now, things change. We don't have time to
          debate this.

                    ALISON
          What? No. But no, I'm not comfortable
          with that. I'm not.

                    BEN
          No. Would you please just listen to her?

                    DR. KUNI
          Fine. Do what you want to do.

                    BEN
          Whoa, whoa, whoa, what?

                    DR. KUNI
          Should I leave? Do you want to be the
          doctor? Because I really don't need to be
          here.

                    BEN
          No. What we want is to take a second to
          talk about our options, okay? That's all
          we want.

                    DR. KUNI
          No. You mean you want to take a second to
          tell me how to do my job. My job is to
          get that baby out safely. Or I can go
          home! You just let me know. You be the
          doctor.

                    BEN
          Can we talk outside in the hall for a
          second?

INT. HOSPITAL - HALLWAY

Ben and Dr. Kuni stand in the hallway.

> DR. KUNI
> That woman is a control freak, and she
> needs to let go and let me do my job.

> BEN
> Look, she's just having a hard time
> because her and her doctor had a very
> specific birth plan. And they wanted it
> to be a very special experience.

> DR. KUNI
> Okay. if you want a special experience,
> go to a Jimmy Buffet concert. We have a
> new birth plan: Get the baby out safely.

> BEN
> Look, man, will you help us out? I have
> no idea what I'm doing. You can be as big
> a dick to me as you want. Just be nice to
> her, man. That's all I ask. Just please
> be nice to her.

Ben's stomach GROWLS loudly.

> DR. KUNI
> Are you okay?

> BEN
> I think so.

> DR. KUNI
> I'm sorry. Let's start fresh.

> BEN
> Thank you, man.

> DR. KUNI
> This is healthy. This is good. I think
> we're bonding.

INT. HOSPITAL ROOM

Dr. Kuni and Ben come back into the room.

> DR. KUNI
> Alison, I apologize for being a little
> brash, but if you're okay with it, it's
> rather important we break the bag and
> give you some medicine to speed things
> up. Because once the bag is broken, I
> don't want there to be an infection.

> ALISON
> Whatever. Do what you have to do.

Dr. Kuni exits.

> ALISON (cont'd)
> (whispering to Ben)
> Oh, my God. What a nightmare that guy is.

                    BEN
I know, I know. Look, I talked to him. I
think he'll be more cool now.

                    ALISON
I'm so sorry I broke up with you.

                    BEN
You really don't need to be. And you
know, I knew you'd give me another shot.
I figured it'd be a lot sooner than this,
you know?

                    ALISON
I was just in such a panic from all of
this. And watching Debbie and Pete
together, and my ass got so fat.

                    BEN
No, no.

                    ALISON
It did. I just never, for one minute,
thought that the guy who got me pregnant
would actually be the right guy for me.

                    BEN
Me neither.

                    ALISON
I guess he is.

INT. HOSPITAL - HALLWAY

Martin and Jonah wheel around the corner in wheelchairs.

                    JONAH
All right, Martin, who am I?

      (impersonating Stephen Hawking)
People think I'm smart because I speak in
a robot voice.

                    MARTIN
Stephen Hawking.

                    JONAH
      (impersonating Stephen Hawking)
I fuck my nurse with my ever-expanding
cock.

      (stops impersonation)
All right. Let's murderball. Come here!
I'm going to murderball you!

Jonah kicks Martin's wheelchair over.

                    MARTIN
Oh, fuck.

                    JONAH
Stay down!

                    MARTIN
Jonah, you shithead!

INT. HOSPITAL ROOM

Debbie and Pete come into the room. Pete holds a camcorder.

                    DEBBIE
          Hi. I can't believe I go out of town and
          this happens.

                    ALISON
          I know.

                    DEBBIE
          I'm sorry, but I'm not going anywhere.

                    ALISON
          Screw Legoland.

                    PETE
          All right, how do you want this? You want
          this over the shoulder? I can do whatever
          you want. I can get in there. Kind of
          Spike Lee angles.

                    ALISON
          No, you can shoot the waiting room. That
          would be great.

                    DEBBIE
               (to Ben)
          Well, thank you. I've got it from here.

                    ALISON
          Debbie.

                    BEN
               (to Debbie)
          Can I talk to you in the hall for a
          second?

                    DEBBIE
          Why?

INT. HOSPITAL - HALLWAY

Ben and Debbie talk in the hallway alone.

                    BEN
          I'd like to be in there with
          Alison...without you.

                    DEBBIE
          Okay. I understand how you feel, but this
          isn't up to you.

                    BEN
          Look, Debbie, you are high off your ass
          if you think you're coming into that
          room. If you take one step towards that
          door, I will tell security there's a
          crazy chick in a pink dress snatching up
          babies. Okay? So don't even try to come
          into that room. That's my room now. That
          little area with the Pepsi
          machine...that's your area. My room. Your
          area. Stay in your area. Stay out of my
          room. Back the fuck off.

INT. HOSPITAL - WAITING ROOM

Debbie sits down in a seat next to Pete.

                    PETE
          What are you doing here?

                    DEBBIE
          He just kicked me out. He told me to
          leave. But I guess it's good, right? He
          said he's going to take care of her. He
          really seems on his game. I think he's
          going to be a good dad. I think I like
          him. Thank God.

                    PETE
          I wish I'd gotten that on tape.

INT. HOSPITAL ROOM

Alison is in labor. She is PANTING.

                    ALISON
          Go! Holy shit, almighty! Oh, shit, this
          really hurts!

                    DR. KUNI
          Ah, I see we're well on our way.

                    ALISON
          I want the epidural! Okay? Give me the
          epidural!

                    BEN
          Give it to her. Give her the epidural,
          okay?

                    ALISON
          Okay?

                    BEN
          Give it to her now.

                    DR. KUNI
          Alison, we're past the point of an
          epidural. The cervix is fully dilated.

                    ALISON
          No, seriously, I want an epidural! I know
          there's time!

                    DR. KUNI
          We can't give you the epidural.

                    ALISON
          Take the time! I'll make sure it doesn't
          come out! I'll stop pushing.

                    BEN
          We have time.

                    ALISON
          I'll stop, oh, please, please, please!

                    BEN
          Just do it, please!

                    DR. KUNI
          I'm sorry. We have no time. We're going
          to just have to do this the all natural
          way, okay? The way you wanted to do it.
          Okay? Ready?

                    ALISON
          Okay.

                    DR. KUNI
          Here comes another contraction, okay? I
          want you to push. Okay, ready? Good,
          good, good.

                    ALISON
          I feel everything! Oh, my God! It's
          happening.

                    SAMUEL
          Maybe we can take it down just a little.
          I think you're going to scare the other
          pregnant women.

                    ALISON
          Are you fucking kidding me? Are you
          kidding me?

INT. HOSPITAL - WAITING ROOM

Alison's SHRIEKING is heard in the waiting room.

                    JAY
          Jesus.

                    JONAH
          Oh. This is messed up. Something's wrong
          in there.

                    JASON
          No, no. I mean, granted, gynecology's
          only a hobby of mine, but it sounds to me
          like she's crowning. Is that right, Deb?

                    DEBBIE
          Yeah. That's what it sounds like for
          everyone. Everyone goes through this.

                    JAY
          No, I disagree with you. That sounds
          terrible. I'm going to go sneak a peek,
          see if there's anything I can do.

Jay goes to Alison's room.

INT. HOSPITAL ROOM

Alison is in agony. Ben, Dr. Kuni and nurses are hunched
around her.

                    DR. KUNI
          It's crowning! I'm seeing the head!

                    ALISON
          Oh, God. Honey, what does it look like,
          Ben?

Been peers down between Alison's legs.

We actually see the crowning shot as the baby's head is being pushed out of Alison's vagina.

                  BEN
    Oh, God.

                  ALISON
    What?

                  BEN
    You don't want to see it. You don't want--

                  ALISON
    No, I want to see it!

                  BEN
    It's beautiful. You don't want to,
    though.

                  ALISON
    No, I want to see...

A nurse holds a mirror for Alison. She sees the actual crowning shot.

                  ALISON (cont'd)
    ...it! Oh, God! Oh, God!

                  DR. KUNI
    Okay, we're almost home! One, two--

Jay bursts in.

                  JAY
    You okay in here?

Jay sees the crowning shot.

                  JAY (cont'd)
    Jesus!

                  ALISON
    Get out!

                  JAY
    Yeah, okay.

INT. HOSPITAL - WAITING ROOM

Jay solemnly returns to his chair.

                  JASON
    You all right, buddy?

                  JAY
    One sec.

                  JONAH
    What did it look like?

                    JAY
          I shouldn't have gone in there. Don't go
          in there. Promise me you don't go in
          there.

                    JONAH
          Me go in there? That's the last fucking
          place I want to go. Like I'm going to go
          in there. Try getting a boner now.

Jason beams at Debbie.

                    JASON
          What's up Deb?

                    DEBBIE
          Hey.

Pete looks at Debbie.

INT. HOSPITAL ROOM

The birth is still in progress.

                    DR. KUNI
          Push. One, two, three.

                    ALISON
          Oh, God!

                    DR. KUNI
          You've passed the shoulders. One more big
          push. Good.

The baby comes out. Dr. Kuni cleans it up.

                    ALISON
          Oh, Ben. I did it.

                    BEN
          You did it.

                    ALISON
          It's out.

                    BEN
          You did it. Oh, my God, you did it.

Dr. Kuni hands the baby to Alison.

                    ALISON
          Hi, baby. I love you, Ben.

                    BEN
          I love you so much, too. Oh, my God.

                    DR. KUNI
          Congratulations, you two. Beautiful.

                    ALISON
          Thank you.

                    DR. KUNI
          You did so great. You were amazing.

                    ALISON
          Pretty baby.

                    BEN
          You got out. You made it out. Welcome.

INT. HOSPITAL - WAITING ROOM

                    MARTIN
          You ever get so bored you just stare at
          your balls?

                    JONAH
          I bet you do, late John Lennon.

                    MARTIN
          Here we go again.

                    DEBBIE
               (whispering to Pete)
          Who is that? Is that Ben's rabbi? Is he
          the one who cuts the penis?

                    PETE
          I think it's Matisyahu.

                    MARTIN
          Awesome.

                    JASON
          You want out of the bet?

                    MARTIN
          I want out of the bet.

                    JASON
          You know what you have to say. Just say
          it, man. I think now is the time.

                    MARTIN
          "Jason, you're the master."

                    JASON
          You heard it, right?

                    JAY
          Yeah.

                    JASON
          All right. You're out of the bet. You're
          done.

Martin hugs Jason.

                    JASON (cont'd)
          Your face smells like an old man's balls.

                    MARTIN
          Thank you.

INT. HOSPITAL ROOM

Debbie and Pete come to check in on Alison.

                    DEBBIE
          Oh, my God. Hello. My goodness. She's
          beautiful. She's beautiful. I love you,
          Ben.

                    BEN
          I love you, Debbie.

                    DEBBIE
               (to Pete)
          We're going to have another baby.

                    PETE
          Okay.

Pete turns the camera on himself and shakes his head "no."

                    DEBBIE
          Hello, baby.

INT. HOSPITAL - WAITING ROOM

Ben enters the waiting room to talk to the guys.

                    BEN
          Gentlemen, it's a girl!

                    THE GUYS
          Ohhhhhhh!

                    BEN
          Yeah!

They all hug.

                    JAY
          We got a daughter! Mazel Tov!

                    JASON
          Congratulations, Daddy!

                    JAY
          We got a beautiful little girl!

                    BEN
          Let's meet her! She's awesome.

                    JAY
          A beautiful little girl!

                    JASON
          Let's meet her. Aw.

INT. HOSPITAL ROOM - LATER

Alison sleeps while Ben holds the baby. Everyone else has
gone home.

                    BEN
               (to the baby)
          And then your mommy said, "Just do it,
          already," which was very confusing to
          Daddy. So I listened to the most literal
          translation of that and I just did it,
          already. What would you do?
               (MORE)

                         BEN (cont'd)
          Don't tell Mommy, but it was the smartest
          thing I ever did, listening to her,
          because now you're here. Isn't that nice?
          I think it is.

EXT. HOSPITAL - DAY

Ben and a Nurse push Alison and the baby in a wheelchair.

I/E ALISON'S CAR

Ben drives while Alison and the baby are in the back seat.

                         ALISON
          I hope your apartment's big enough for
          the three of us.

                         BEN
          It definitely is. That's why I got one in
          East LA. The rent. It's huge! The only
          thing is we have to decide if we're going
          to be Crips or Bloods before we get
          there.

                         ALISON
          Well, I look good in red.

                         BEN
          I look good in blue. The fighting
          continues. We could just throw off
          everyone and become Latin Kings.

                         ALISON
          Yeah.

                         BEN
          We both look good in gold.

                         ALISON
          Good choice. I would yell at you about
          driving so slow, except the baby's here.

                         BEN
          No, these guys can honk all they want. I
          ain't going faster than twelve. It might
          take us around three hours to get home,
          though.

The car moves slowly down the highway with a line of cars
waiting behind them.

FADE OUT.

AFTERWORD

BY CHARLYNE YI

Hi _____,

My name is Charlyne Yi. Um. I played the character of Jodi in the movie you just read: *Knocked Up*. I don't know why I'm here...writing this...right now. Judd asked me to. He really didn't give me much direction, just said something about writing about my experience on the movie. OH YEAH! I almost forgot, today is Sept 12, 2007. Thought that might be an interesting fact as to when YOU are reading this in time. In comparison to where I am in time. Ha, I feel like Marty McFly writing to Doc Brown. I wish I had something important to say about your future. Oh! You know that thing you've been holding off? Well, hold off no longer! I saw the future and you end up an old fart. So you better do something. Or else. You'll regret it. For the rest of your life. Forever. Really. I'm not horsing around.

Sincerely,

Charlyne from the past

Okay, here I go:

HOW I GOT THE PART:

Well, I originally auditioned for a girl that Alison runs into when shopping with Ben for baby clothes & I also read for a doctor's receptionist. I felt like I would never get either of those roles and was really

surprised when I got called in to come in and audition in front of Judd & the guys.

When I came in Seth & Evan said they had seen me perform before and thought I was funny, and that made me even scareder to audition because I didn't want them to think I sucked. I started to read. I'm a very poor reader, took Hooked on Phonics as a kid. So there I was jittering as I read coldly without knowing that the character was supposed to be stoned. I didn't know how to act high.

I think I kept covering my face with my script because I was laughing because I was very uncomfortable—not because it was funny. That's when Judd told me to get rid of my script and just improvise. I had to improvise with Seth. His back was turned to the guys, but his face was looking directly at mine. I wasn't saying anything funny, and Seth's face kept expressing pain. Finally I said one thing and we started to laugh. I don't remember what I said. But it was such a relief I said it because I could leave with an upbeat ending. I said thank you to Alison (the casting director) and waved goodbye and I think accidentally hit her. I thought for sure I wasn't going to get the part.

Improvising with Seth:

MY EXPERIENCE:

Oh boy.... where do I start?

The night before my first day of shooting, my car had died in downtown LA and a crazy man robbed me with a gun pointing at me from inside his pants (near his crotch area). After we caught the bad guy, I had to talk to the cops and file a report. Then I got myself and my car towed back to Fontana (where I lived at the time). Went to bed for 3 hours. Borrowed my mom's car and drove to Knott's Berry Farm from there.

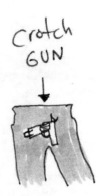

Crotch
GUN
↓

With that happening the night before, I was a lot more nervous than usual. It was quite an uncomfortable situation because I really suck at talking to people because I'm terrified of them as well as roller coasters. I didn't really talk to anyone this day. I was much more of an observer.

We were waiting for Jay Baruchel to come to ride the roller coaster with us. And everybody kept talking about how terrified Jay was of going on it. I was so confused because I saw Jason Segel, and he seemed very calm and was laughing it up with the guys (I thought Jay was short for Jason). And then came a guy who paced around, with his hands in his pits, and eyebrows that tilted oh so sadly. That was Jay.

We all got on the rollercoaster and afterwards the guys threw up. I didn't throw up because I hadn't eaten before I went on. Instead, I dry-heaved A LOT. It was painful and gross. An intense day for Charlyne Yi.

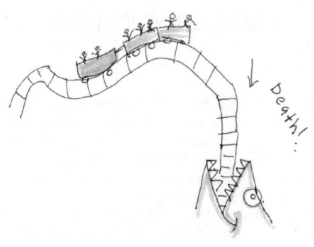

death!

I was never sure how long they were going to keep me. They ended up bringing me back a month later. And kept me for a whole week. I was only supposed to work ONE day. A week bought me enough time to storm up the courage to actually talk to the (good?) fellas.

BEST LAUGH IN THE UNIVERSE

SETH ROGEN

My first thoughts of the guys:
*Martin = Scary
*Seth = # 1 laugh
*Jason = Best Friends forever
*Jay = Scared of roller coasters
*Katie = Tough broad—my kind of gal
*Jonah = intimidating

In the end, Martin actually became one of my closest friends. We bowl together. Seth won an award for best laugh in the universe— and it's made out of GOLD (top-notch, I'd concur). Jason and I don't hang out at all—but one day I'll make him my best friend and we'll wear those cool necklaces with the heart that splits in half and reads "Best" on one half and "friend" on the other. Jay... is afraid of roller coasters... till this very day. Katie is tougher than ever but still manages to be kindest of all creatures. And whenever I see Jonah now, he threatens me with a hug because he knows I hate them, which makes him intimidating.

BEST FRIENDS

if martin and I had a baby

THOUGHT I WAS GOING TO GET FIRED:

The day we shot the scene where Alison meets Ben's roommates and my character is intrusive and annoying:

Sound! Rolling! Action! —Wait a minute... CUT!

I was a nervous wreck, sweating like a madman. I had said my lines as if I were reading. Very stilted. I remember thinking when Judd yelled cut and popped into the room, "Oh man, he's totally going to fire me, this is not good. My part isn't even essential to the movie. They could just cut it. Or fire me. He's gonna fire me, isn't he?"

Judd rubbed his forehead and said, "Uh... can you do what you did at your audition?" And I replied, "I don't remember." And then Judd told me to forget about the script, to just improvise and have fun, and that he was going to let the film roll for like 10 minutes and to just keep going.

And we forgot about the script and just had fun improvising. And it was fun. And it felt good. Real good.

ON SET:

It was unbelievably hot in Northridge. 119 to be exact. I remember looking at the ground as I walked to avoid the mighty sun from killing my eyes, I could see liquid smacking the ground. It was my sweat. I had never sweated like that in my life before. The heat. It made everybody pretty exhausted. And so during down time Jason, Jay, and I would lie in Ben's bedroom and talk on the bed. I don't know how it happened, but one day we all fell asleep. It was a deep sleep. When I woke up I was absolutely terrified because I completely forgot where I was—so the first thing I saw was Jason snoring in my face! The wind from his nose woke me up. Still a little startled, I rolled over and then BAM! Jay was on my other side. I think somebody took a picture. I probably looked like some dirty broad sleeping around.

THE DRIVE TO AND FROM THE VALLEY:

At the time I wasn't really living in Los Angeles. I would sometimes sleep in my car or couch-surf between friends' places. So when I was there, the drive wasn't so far. When I wasn't and didn't have a place to stay, I'd go back to Fontana with my parents. The drives from there were pretty long especially because my car would always break down. It's nuts because I'm so soooo lucky and thankful for getting this job because that's the thing that allowed me to have enough to move to LA. I've almost been living in a real place for a year now! It's wonderful.

CRAFT SERVICES:

The food was amazing. I never experienced anything like it before. It was like a really amazing buffet. Oh so yummy.

WHAT WAS IT LIKE WHEN THE MOVIE CAME OUT?

I was really excited to be part of a movie and see how it came out. I felt like the resulting movie came out a lot different from the script. I loved Leslie Mann in the movie. Sigh. She almost made me cry.

When I saw it for the first time, it was at the premiere. I took my mom. I remember when I saw my big fat face on the big screen it was overwhelming. I had never seen my face so big before. I was a booger in comparison to screen me. And my voice... so loud. I don't know if I'll be able to get used to watching myself without feeling sick.

me on the big screen

136

me sick after I saw myself (not really) on the big screen

The premiere was nuts. I remember going down the red carpet. And it was terrifying. A bunch of photographers yelling very aggressively trying to speak over one another, "SMILE! CHARLYNE! NO, LOOK THIS WAY! NO, THIS WAY! SMILE! SMILE!!!" All of them fighting for my attention. I couldn't take it and yelled, "Whoa, guys! Why are you yelling at me?!" And flailed my arms in the air. And realized I had some muscles I had been meaning to show off. And just tried to have fun flexing because I'm not fond of taking pictures and it was already an uncomfortable thing having it be that everybody was yelling. Instead of trying to make myself smile or look nice, I said, "The hell with it! (flex) Take this, America!"

Charlyne Yi on the red carpet

muscles shining through

RED CARPET

SINCE THE MOVIE'S COME OUT, HAS YOUR LIFE CHANGED?

Not drastically. Why do you ask? Oh.

I don't know how to answer this question. Hmm... well...

Once in a while I'll get recognized. But it's almost always incredibly awkward.

One time after a show I was talking to my friends in front of the UCB theatre and a guy interrupted us and said, "Hey!" and stared at me intensely. And I said, "Hi." Even though I was scared. Long pause. I suppose he was analyzing my face. And he asked, "Are you an actor?" And I said, "Kind of." 'Cause I'm not really. And he said, "*Knocked Up*?" and I said, "Yeah." "You played Jodi?" I nodded yes. And then he just kept staring for a very long time. Blink. Blink. Blink. I could hear him breathing. It was weird. "Are you sure?" he questioned me again. I replied nervously, "I think so?" Mini pause. And without saying anything else, he walked away. I don't think he believed me.

Or some people will come up to me excited and I'll get nervous and start to laugh, and then they'll say I'm exactly like my character. One time I responded by saying, "Yeah, we kind of look alike and sound the same." That was my nervous attempt to try to engage in a conversation and make a joke. But no one laughed except me. The end.

One thing that's really neat is that I do these live shows, and a group of people from like North Carolina (or somewhere near there) were visiting LA and they had looked me up on the Internet because of *Knocked Up* and decided to come to one of my shows. So strange how the movie intertwined with the stuff I do in my regular life.

Oh! Ha, my little sister told me that at her

school they had celebrity day and she dressed up as me. I hadn't found out till it happened, otherwise I would've stopped her. She told me no one but one of her friends knew who she was supposed to be. And that a boy came up to her and asked her, "What are you supposed to be? A hobo?" And my little sister was so mad, but confused-mad, because she didn't know what a hobo was.

ET GROWN UP

My friend Nick Jasenovec said when he's rich he's going to ~~sutgerally~~ get surgery on his butt to make ~~it horizon~~ his crack horizontal so it could smile. I told him d'd buy him denchers for it.

139

JUDD APATOW CREATES COMEDY WITH A LITTLE HELP FROM HIS FRIENDS

BY SARAH VANCE

Writer-director-producer Judd Apatow knows that the premise for his new film, *Knocked Up,* may not be the most original idea for a comedy. "Every story that has ever been told has already been done as well as it can be done on *The Simpsons,*" Apatow says. "So it's really more about putting your own spin on the story, and I've come to believe that good story ideas are very simple, and the rest is all about the execution. For a long time, I thought you needed a big, high-concept idea or an intricate plot. But now I think that if I'm really honest, any idea can be funny and interesting, especially if I'm not afraid to go all the way with a confessional style."

As writer-director-producer of the smash hit *The 40-Year-Old Virgin,* Apatow has honed his comedy writing skills with the best in the business. "A great lesson that Garry Shandling taught me when I was working on *The Larry Sanders Show* was that whenever we were really stuck on a story beat, he would say, 'Well, what would really happen? What would Hank do?' And then we'd know where to go next."

After paying his dues as a stand-up comic, Apatow went to the USC School of Cinema-Television for a year and a half. But when he landed his first job in television in 1991, Apatow started at the top as the showrunner for *The Ben Stiller Show.* "Ben and I had heard that HBO was looking for a sketch comedy show, so we came up with this idea. I had no idea what I was doing," Apatow says with a laugh. "I'd sit in my office listening to relaxation tapes every day to deal with the stress from not knowing what

Reprinted by kind permission of the author. Originally published in the May/June 2007 edition of *Script* magazine.

I was doing. But that's kind of the charm of the show. It was clearly made by people who are figuring it all out as they go and are too dumb to do something that has been done before."

Inspired by the films of Albert Brooks and *Second City TV*, the writers of *The Ben Stiller Show* took parody to a new level by raising the production values. "When we did parody, the sketches really looked like the movie we were making fun of. Ben loved the idea of making our sketches exactly like the movie we were parodying, down to the point that we'd often use the same locations."

Still, *The Ben Stiller Show* struggled over two years to find an audience. "I've always tried to do things that are original," Apatow points out. "I felt like the work would be better if I hadn't seen it a hundred times before, so I've tried to avoid what has been traditionally done—which is probably why so much of my work in television was cancelled so quickly."

After *The Ben Stiller Show*, Apatow landed two jobs in television—writing for *The Larry Sanders Show* as a consultant and writing for *The Critic*, an adult cartoon created by Mike Reiss and Al Jean of *The Simpsons*. "*The Critic* was produced by James Brooks, so I was lucky enough to be in a few situations where we broke stories with him," Apatow says. "The best film school education you can get is watching James Brooks work through a story problem. The rest of the week, I would do that with Garry Shandling. So just by paying attention and thinking carefully about why they were making the choices they did, I was able to begin to understand how to tell stories."

Apatow knows that his lifestyle has forced his writing style to change over the years. "Before I was married, I'd stay home and watch television all day, procrastinate until 7:00 or 8:00 at night, and then I would write for two or three hours. That was a successful writing day—10 or 12 hours of procrastination and not showering, followed by a short burst of creativity. Now that I'm married with children, I've learned how to schedule my writing. I've tried everything. Sometimes, I write at night after the phone stops ringing, and every once in a while, I'll go to the office early before the phone starts ringing and try to get some pages written before the madness of the day begins."

With time and experience, Apatow believes his writing process has become fairly simple. "I take a few months to ramble out some ideas. I don't outline at first. I just write down tons of ideas because I know as soon as I outline, I'm going to get somewhat locked into that story; so I try not to lay out the story too quickly. Then I outline for a month or two, and once I'm happy with the outline, I try to write more than seven pages a day. I do that every day until I get a draft done. I usually do a draft in a month or two, and then I go through 10 or 20 pages of rewriting every day. When I get through that pass, I try to do a table read. My goal is always to get to a table read as quickly as possible. Once I hear it out loud, then I know what needs to happen."

Apatow refers to his first draft as a "vomit pass," a draft of a screenplay that he writes quickly with a lot of his story ideas coming out as a result of not judging himself too harshly. "Then I do a separate pass where I'm really tough on the script."

As a feature-film producer and a television showrunner, Apatow has overseen a lot of other writers. "I've seen the people who try to be creative and critical at the same time, and they're the people who take a year and a half to write a draft. I'm all for writing a draft very quickly."

A big fan of "how to write" books, Apatow believes the theories about the differences between right-brain and left-brain thinking. "You have one side of your brain that's very creative, and one side that's very mathematical and analytical. I think it's helpful to separate pure, creative time from the time when I'm being critical of my own work. I think a lot of ideas come from your unconscious, and you should let them flow and then figure out the meaning of them afterward."

After he collaborated with Steve Carell on the script of *The 40-Year-Old Virgin* and Nicholas Stoller on *Fun with Dick and Jane*, *Knocked Up* is the first feature-film script that Apatow wrote by himself. "I really like writing with other people. I think especially for comedy writing, it's difficult not to have other people around to laugh when you think of something that you hope is really funny. But I decided to write *Knocked Up* alone because the idea was very personal, and I wanted it to remain pure."

These days, Apatow has a seasoned troupe of actors that he likes to collaborate with when he's developing new ideas. "It's just so rare to find people who are funny, talented and speak your language. I try to write an okay first draft, and then as early as possible, I cast the movie so I can have the actors involved in the rewrite. We do table reads and rehearsals, and I do drafts based on what happens in those rehearsals. But as soon as we start shooting, all bets are off. We always start with the script, but everyone knows that I expect the actors to make a contribution and take it to the next level on the day of filming. Sometimes we stick very close to the script and we're happy to see that it works. And other times, it feels stiff. I think a lot of comedy feels scripted, so I'm always looking at how the actors adjust the words to make it more comfortable. Or sometimes they just say something completely different that surprises the other actors, and then you get some very genuine reactions and interactions. If you understand emotionally what the arc of the scene is, you can change some of the details in the moment to something that feels a little more immediate."...

Knocked Up stars Seth Rogen and Katherine Heigl and has two great supporting performances from the familiar faces of Paul Rudd and Leslie Mann, Apatow's wife. "I always believed that Seth could carry a movie. While Seth and Paul only had one scene together in *The 40-Year-Old Virgin*, I felt like their pairing was an untapped combination. And because I know Leslie so well, I knew I could get things out of her that another director couldn't.

"*Knocked Up* is kind of a beauty and [the] beast story," Apatow laughs. "The truth is that Seth's adorable and the audience falls in love with him. But in reality, the audience can understand why she would think this is a horrible mistake. 'What if some idiot pothead got you pregnant? What would you do?'

"My original idea for the script wasn't that the girl had to be gorgeous. But when Katherine Heigl got the part, we had to address the fact that Seth Rogen was dating someone way out of his league. During the editing process, I remember writing on a scrap of paper that the story was about how someone falls in love with someone else before they do. That's their conflict."

Knocked Up also features a surprisingly hilarious cameo by *American Idol* host Ryan Seacrest. "It's very rare when you find someone who will satirize what he does and his persona. Ryan was completely game. That scene could not have been more fun to shoot," Apatow adds. "We had a script, but as we were shooting, I was yelling out things for him to say. I'd scream out, 'Say I'm more famous than all of these kids.' And he'd say it. He'd just crack up and go for it."...

After a writing-directing project, Apatow may need some time off. "I like writing and directing, but after I do it, I need a year or two to recover. It's fun, but it's also very stressful to feel that kind of pressure for so long," Apatow says. "It's also very inspiring to work with other writers and directors, to pitch jokes and be supportive in whatever way I can. Then I find the courage to want to direct another movie myself."

Apatow's hugely successful comedies may seem to be commercially calculated blends of lowbrow slacker humor and sweet chick-flick romance, but he is quick to point out that it isn't a conscious act. "I've never used the word 'romantic' in a sentence in my life," he laughs. "I just write stories about the kind of guy I was in my late teens and early 20s. So the stories that I end up telling are about funny people or slackers because that's what I know. I don't really know how an Alaskan Eskimo behaves, so I don't even try. But I do have an ability to capture the behavior of some knuckleheads that I've known or that I was. And in certain situations, I guess it's kind of entertaining to see them learn the lessons they need to learn to get to the next place in their lives."

CAST AND CREW CREDITS

UNIVERSAL PICTURES PRESENTS
An APATOW Production

"KNOCKED UP"

SETH ROGEN   KATHERINE HEIGL   PAUL RUDD   LESLIE MANN
JAY BARUCHEL   JONAH HILL   JASON SEGEL   MARTIN STARR

Music by	Editors	Executive Producers
LOUDON WAINWRIGHT	BRENT WHITE	SETH ROGEN
JOE HENRY	CRAIG ALPERT	EVAN GOLDBERG

Music Supervisor
JONATHAN KARP

Production Designer
JEFFERSON SAGE

Produced by
JUDD APATOW
SHAUNA ROBERTSON
CLAYTON TOWNSEND

Costume Designer
DEBRA McGUIRE

Director of Photography
ERIC EDWARDS

Written and Directed by
JUDD APATOW

CAST

Ben Stone . . . . Seth Rogen
Alison Scott . . . . Katherine Heigl
Pete . . . . Paul Rudd
Debbie . . . . Leslie Mann
Jason . . . . Jason Segel
Jay . . . . Jay Baruchel
Jonah . . . . Jonah Hill
Martin . . . . Martin Starr
Jodi . . . . Charlyne Yi
Charlotte . . . . Iris Apatow
Sadie . . . . Maude Apatow
Alison's Mom . . . . Joanna Kerns
Ben's Dad . . . . . Harold Ramis
Jack . . . . Alan Tudyk
Jill . . . . Kristen Wiig
Brent . . . . Bill Hader
Dr. Kuni . . . . Ken Jeong
Club Doorman . . . . Craig Robinson
Dr. Pellagrino . . . . Tim Bagley
Dr. Howard . . . . . . Loudon Wainwright
Dr. Howard's Nurse . . . Stephanie Mnookin
Male Nurse . . . . Adam Scott
Dr. Angelo . . . . J.P. Manoux
Female Doctor . . . . Mo Collins
Young Doctor . . . . B.J. Novak
Wardrobe Lady . . . . Tami Sagher
Alison's Friends . . . . Brianna Lynn Brown
Catherine Reitman
Nick Thune
Fantasy Baseball Guys . . . . . . Paul Feig
Ben Meyerson
Wayne Federman

Dr. Pellagrino's Nurse . . . Melinda Bennett
Club Bartender . . . . Matt McKane
Ben's Boss . . . . Steven Brill
Maria . . . . Ana Mercedes
Maternity Nurse at Desk . . Nadine Griffith
Delivery Nurse . . . . . . Diane Schaller
Jonah's Girlfriend . . . . . . Emersen Riley
Lap Dancers . . . . Stormy Daniels
Nautica Thorn
Real Estate Agent . . . . Mary Brill
Daughter in Waiting Room . . Lolita Mastrolia
Father in Waiting Room . . Joseph T. Mastrolia
Lamaze Instructor . . . . . . Tracy Hartley
Record Store Customer . . Jeffrey L. Wilson
Stunt Coordinator . . . . . Malosi Leonard
Stunt Player . . . . Matthew Leonard

CREW

Written and Directed by . . . . Judd Apatow
Produced by . . . . '. Judd Apatow
Shauna Robertson
Clayton Townsend
Executive Producers . . . . . . Seth Rogen
Evan Goldberg
Director of Photography . . . . Eric Edwards
Production Designer . . . . . Jefferson Sage
Editors . . . . Brent White
Craig Alpert
Costume Designer . . . . Debra McGuire
Music Supervisor . . . . . . Jonathan Karp
Music by . . . . Loudon Wainwright
Joe Henry

Casting by . . . . Allison Jones
Unit Production Manager
. . . . Clayton Townsend
First Assistant Director . . . Matt Rebenkoff
Second Assistant Director. . Courtenay Miles
Additional Editor. . . . . Melissa Bretherton
Production Supervisor . . Gary R. Wordham
Art Director. . . . . Lauren Polizzi
Set Decorator . . . . Chris Spellman
Set Designers . . . . Elizabeth Lapp
Alicia Maccarone
Masako Masuda
Leadman . . . . Mark Weissenfluh
Art Department Coordinator
. . . . , Ari Jacobs Libarkin
Camera/Steadicam Operator
. . . . Peter Rosenfeld
Camera Operator . . . . Nils Benson
First Assistant Camera. . . . . Scott Rathner
Paul Horn
Second Assistant Camera. . . Peter Geraghty
Paul Tilden
Film Loader . . . . Greg Kurtz
Sound Mixer . . . . . . David MacMillian
Boom Operators . . . . . Jack M. Nitzsche
Harrison Marsh
Sound Utility . . . . Kevin Patterson
Production Coordinator. . Barrett J. Klausman
Property Master. . . . . . . Sean Mannion
Assistant Property Master . . Michael Glynn
Assistant Props . . . . Bert Smith
On Set Dresser . . . . Jon Nicholson
Set Dressers . . . . Jack Blanchard
Mark Green
Scott G. Jones
Adam B. Kirby
Anthony Klaiman
Nashon Petrushkin
Buyer . . . . Kristen Gassner
Costume Supervisors. . . Joseph T. Mastrolia
Katrina Mastrolia
Key Set Costumer—Women . . Jennifer Iizuka
Key Set Costumer—Men
. . . . Michael A. Russell
Costumer . . . . Catherine Hahn
Costume Buyer . . . . . Winifred Clements
Key Hairstylist . . . . Thomas Real
Hairstylist. . . . . Nanxy Tong-Heater
Additional Hairstylists . . Pauletta Lewis-Irwin
Charlotte Parker
Key Makeup Artist . . . . . Ann Pala Taylor
Assistant Makeup Artist. . Kathleen Freeman
Prosthetic Design & Application
. . . . Matthew Mungle

Prosthetic Application . . . . Clinton Wayne
Ruth Haney
Additional Makeup Artists. . Corina C. Duran
Alexis Walker
Chief Lighting Technician
. . . . Donald L. Bixby, Jr.
Best Boy Electric. . . . . . . Marc Marino
Set Lighting Technicians . . . Jason Brunelle
Jimmy Ellis
Gordon Eto
Earl D. Gayer
William Streit
Chris Weigand
Rigging Gaffer . . . . Craig A. Brink
Best Boy Rigging Electric. . David Diamond
Rigging Electrics . . . . Brandon Ainsworth
Randy Babchuck
Kevin Cadwallader
Gustavo Graciano
Glen Magers
Marc Salter
Mark Wostak
Key Grip . . . . Doug Cowden
Best Boy Grip . . . . Walter Royle
Dolly Grips . . . . Gary A. Williams
Anthony Thomas
Grips. . . . . Bruce Byall
Shannon Deats
Sam Escobar
Grant Goza
Eric Leach
Matt Jackson
Tomy Sommo
Teague Uva
Jeffrey L. Wilson
Key Rigging Grip . . . . . . Brady Majors
Rigging Best Boy Grip . . Caleb R. Nelson
Rigging Grips . . . . Craig Bilodeau
Pete Johnson
Cory Peavler
Edward Pickrell
Lance Robinson
Bill Schwocho
Hannes Steixner
Special Effects Supervisor . . . Matt Sweeney
Special Effects Technicians . . . Steve Luport
Lucinda Strub
Script Supervisor . . . . . . Rebecca Asher
Supervising Sound Editor. . George Anderson
Re-Recording Mixers . . . . . Scott Millan
David Parker
Post Production Supervisor . . Lisa Rodgers
Associate Editor. . . . . Scott Davids
1st Film Assistant Editor. . . Ray Neapolitan

Film Assistant Editor . . . . . . Laura Behary
Avid Assistant Editor . . . . . Colin Patton
Editorial Production Assistant . . Jim Carretta
Supervising ADR Editor . . Tammy Fearing
Sound Effects Editor . . . . . Cindy Marty
Dialogue Editor . . . . Joe Schiff
First Assistant Sound Editor . . Cherie Tamai
ADR Assistant Editor . . . . Bill Burns
Assistants to Mr. Apatow . . Andrew Epstein
Greg Cohen
Lisa Yadavaia
Production Accountant . . . . . Mike Revell
1st Assistant Accountant . . . . Eileen Dennis
2nd Assistant Accountants . . Naomi Catalano
Jennifer Jacobs
Payroll Accountant . . . . . Karen M. Fuchs
Construction Accountant . . . Luika Imaoka
Accounting Clerk . . . . . . Erica Gonzales
Post Production Accountant . . James O. Maull
Location Manager . . . . . . Boyd Wilson
Key Assistant Location Managers . . Brad Bell
Jacob Charney
Naomi Motohashi
Assistant Location Manager . . . James Small
Aerial Director of Photography
. . . . David B. Nowell
Helicopter Pilot . . . . . . Peter McKernan
Ground Safety Coordinator . . Lance Strumpf
Casting Assistant . . . . . . Dorian Frankel
Extras Casting . . . . . . Dee Dee Ricketts
Carla Lewis
Tina Kerr
Assistant Production Coordinators . . Selena Carrillo
Brook Worley
Production Secretary . . . . Kate Galbraith
2nd 2nd Assistant Director . . Paul B. Schneider
Set Production Assistants . . Kathryn Tucker
Blake Nabavi
Jadi McCurdy
Marike Jainchill
Office Production Assistants . . Matthew Bass
Michelle Beress
Chase Fein
Stuart Bam
Robbie Woolrich
Art Dept. Production Assistant
. . . . Hunter Woo
Camera Production Assistant . . Dennis Geraghty
Costume Dept. Production Assistants
. . . . Samantha Davis
Michelle Finkelstein
Locations Production Assistants
. . . . Justin Harrold
Jacob Torres

Cast Production Assistants . . Shaun O'Banion
Richard P. Lewis
DGA Trainee . . . . Aaron Critchlow
Construction Coordinator . . Anthony Lattanzio
General Foreman . . . Christopher W. Meyer
Propmaker Foreman . . . . Anthony Godfrey
Labor Foreman . . . . Terry Miller
Plaster Foreman . . . . . Eugenio Quinteru
Paint Foreman . . . . . . David Goldstein
Standby Painter . . . . Bill Hoyt
Drapery Foreman . . . . . Armando Abarca
Greens Foreman . . . . . Tony Castagnola
Transportation Coordinator . . Michael Shannon
Transportation Captain . . . . Oliver Eisinger
Transportation Dispatcher . . . Jayson Chang
D.O.T. Compliance Coordinator
. . . . Julie Sanders
Video Assist . . . . Jay Huntoon
Video Playback . . . . Steve Irwin
Video Playback Operators . . . Eric Roberts
Tom Schurke
Still Photographer . . Suzanne Hanover, SMPSP
Unit Publicist . . . . Deborah Wuliger
Dailies Projectionist . . . . . Casey L. Kamps
Assets . . . . Melody Murray
Caterer . . . . Gala Catering
Food Stylist . . . . Joyce Mannion
Craft Service . . . . Chance P. Tassone
Craft Service Assistant . . . . . Joseph Milito
Studio Teacher . . . . Rhona Gordon
Infant Nurse . . . . Didi Vitale, RN
Set Medic . . . . . . Ericka Bryce Poniewaz
Medical Technical Advisor . . Susie Schelling
ADR Voice Casting . . . Wendy Hoffmann
ADR Voices . . . . Theo Borders
Ranjani Brow
Rachel Crane
Caitlin Cutt
Wendy Hoffmann
Scott Menville
Shani Pride
Christina Rodgers
Justin Shenkarow
Shane Sweet
Hans Tester
Tyler Zaentz
ADR Mixer . . . . Greg Steele
ADR Recordist . . . . . Greg Zimmerman
Dubbing Recordist . . . . . Drew Webster
Foley Artists . . . . Goro Koyama
Caoimhe Doyle
Andy Malcolm
Foley Recording Mixers . . . . Don White
Ron Mellegers

Foley Recording Assistants . . . Anna Malkin
Jenna Dalla Riva
Foley Recorded at
. . . Footsteps Post-Production Sound, Inc.
Executive in Charge of Music for
Universal Pictures . . . . . . Kathy Nelson
Additional Music . . . . . . Lyle Workman
Music Editor . . . . Jonathan Karp
Bass . . . . David Piltch
Drums. . . . . Jay Bellerose
Guitar . . . . Richard Thompson
Guitar . . . . Greg Leisz
Keyboards . . . . Patrick Warren
Score Recorded and Mixed by
. . . . Ryan Freeland
Main Title and Opticals by . . . . . Yard FX
End Titles by. . . Right Lobe Design Group
Digital Intermediate
. . . . . Technicolor Digital Intermediates
Digital Film Colorist. . . . . Jeff Smithwick
Digital Intermediate Producer. . Jimmy Fusil
Negative Cutter. . . . . Gary Burritt
Dolby Sound Consultant . . . . Thom Ehle
Camera Cranes & Dollies by
. . Chapman/Leonard Studio Equipment, Inc.
Visual Effects by. . Perpetual Motion Pictures
Pacific Vision Productions, Inc.

2nd Unit
Director of Photography . . . Josh Bleibtreu
First Assistant Director
. . . . Dawn Massaro-Adams
Second Assistant Director. . Heather Grierson
First Assistant Camera . . . . Don Steinberg
Second Assistant Camera . . . Steven Cueva

SOUNDTRACK ON
CONCORD RECORDS

"SHIMMY SHIMMY YA"
Written by Robert Diggs Jr., Russell Jones
Performed by Ol' Dirty Bastard
Courtesy of Elektra Entertainment Group
By arrangement with Warner Music Group
Film & TV Licensing

"GREY IN L.A."
Written by Loudon Wainwright III
Performed by Loudon Wainwright III

"SANTERIA"
Written by Floyd I. Gaugh IV, Bradley James
Nowell, Eric John Wilson
Performed by Sublime
Courtesy of Geffen Records
Under license from Universal Music Enterprises

"DOUBLE VISION"
Written by Melissa Elias, Jered Gummere,
Brian Case, Nathan Jerde
Performed by The Ponys
Courtesy of Matador Records

"CLUMSY"
Written by Stacy Ferguson, Will Adams,
Bobby Troup
Performed by Fergie
Courtesy of A&M Records
Under license from Universal Music Enterprises

"UP LOUD"
Written by Michael Fratantuno, Terence
Yoshiaki Graves, Brian Lapin
Performed by Transcenders
Courtesy of Transcenders, LLC

"SHAKE"
Written by Richard Jones, Craig Lawson,
Darryl Richardson II
Performed by Trina (featuring Lil Scrappy)
Courtesy of Slip-N-Slide Records/Atlantic
Recording Corp.
By arrangement with Warner Music Group
Film & TV Licensing

"ALL NIGHT"
Written by Stephen Marley, Damian Robert
Nesta Marley, Clement Dodd, Jackie Mittoo
Performed by Damian Marley featuring
Stephen Marley
Courtesy of Universal Records
Under license from Universal Music Enterprises

"SMILE"
Written by Lily Allen, Iyiola Babatunde
Babalola, Darren Emilio Lewis, Clement
Dodd, Jackie Mittoo
Performed by Lily Allen
Courtesy of Capitol Records
Under license from EMI Film & Television
Music

"SWING"
Written by Nathan Holmes, Aaron Fabian
Ngawhika, Demetrius Christian Savelio
Performed by Savage
Courtesy of Dawn Raid Entertainment

"ROCK LOBSTER"
Written by Kate Pierson, Fred Schneider,
Keith Strickland, Cindy Wilson, Ricky
Wilson
Performed by The B-52's
Courtesy of Warner Bros. Records Inc.
By arrangement with Warner Music Group
Film & TV Licensing and
Courtesy of The Island Def Jam Music
Group,
Under license from Universal Music
Enterprises and Courtesy of Man Woman
Together Now, Inc.

"BIGGEST PART OF ME"
Written by David Robert Pack
Performed by Ambrosia
Courtesy of Warner Bros. Records Inc.
By arrangement with Warner Music Group
Film & TV Licensing

"TROPICANA"
Written by Evan Mast, Mike Stroud
Performed by Ratatat
Courtesy of XL Recordings

"RUNNING THE BATH"
Written by Mark Oliver Everett
Performed by Mark Oliver Everett

"POLICE ON MY BACK"
Written by Eddy Grant
Performed by The Clash
Courtesy of Sony BMG Music
Entertainment (UK) Limited
By arrangement with Sony BMG Music
Entertainment

"ALL ALONG THE WATCHTOWER"
Written by Bob Dylan
Performed by DMC
Courtesy of RomenMpire Records/From
Rags 2 Riches Records

"SUNDAY EVENING"
Written by Michael Fratantuno, Terence
Yoshiaki Graves, Brian Lapin
Performed by Transcenders
Courtesy of Transcenders, LLC

"KEEP ON DUBBING"
Written by Horace M. Swaby
Performed by Augustus Pablo
Courtesy of Shanachie Entertainment Corp.

"CONSIDER HER WAYS"
Written by Reggie Moore
Performed by Reggie Moore
Courtesy of Pure Music, Inc.

"BULLCORN"
Written by Robert Ellen
Performed by Goree Carter
Courtesy of Pure Music, Inc.

"LOVE ME"
Written by Jerry Leiber, Mike Stoller
Performed by The Little Willies
Courtesy of Milking Bull Records
Under license from EMI Film & Television
Music

"LULLABY"
Written by Loudon Wainwright III
Performed by Loudon Wainwright III

"KING WITHOUT A CROWN"
Written by Matthew Miller, Josh Werner
Performed by Matisyahu
Courtesy of Epic Records
By arrangement with Sony BMG Music
Entertainment

"LOVE PLUS ONE"
Written by Nick Heyward
Performed by Haircut 100
Courtesy of Sony BMG Music
Entertainment (UK) Limited
By arrangement with Sony BMG Music
Entertainment

"GIRL"
Written by Beck Hansen, John King, Mike
Simpson
Performed by Beck
Courtesy of Interscope Records
Under license from Universal Music Enterprises

"DANGER (BEEN SO LONG)"
Written by Pharrell L. Williams, Chad Hugo,
Michael Tyler
Performed by Mystikal
Courtesy of Jive Records
By arrangement with Sony BMG Music
Entertainment

"SIGN YOUR NAME"
Written by Sananda Maitreya
Performed by Sananda Maitreya fka Terence
Trent D'Arby
Courtesy of Sony BMG Music
Entertainment (UK) Limited
By arrangement with Sony BMG Music
Entertainment

"WISHING WELL"
Written by Sananda Maitreya, Sean Oliver
Performed by Sananda Maitreya fka Terence
Trent D'Arby
Courtesy of Sony BMG Music
Entertainment (UK) Limited
By arrangement with Sony BMG Music
Entertainment

"IF YOU LET ME STAY"
Written by Sananda Maitreya
Performed by Sananda Maitreya fka Terence
Trent D'Arby
Courtesy of Sony BMG Music
Entertainment (UK) Limited
By arrangement with Sony BMG Music
Entertainment

"PUT IT ON"
Written by Bob Marley
Performed by Bob Marley & The Wailers
Courtesy of The Island Def Jam Music
Group
Under license from Universal Music Enterprises

"MANUEL'S GOT A TRAIN TO
CATCH"
Written by Mark Oliver Everett
Performed by Mark Oliver Everett

"TOXIC"
Written by Cathy Dennis, Henrik Jonback,
Christian Karlsson, Pontus Johan Winnberg
Performed by Britney Spears
Courtesy of Jive Records
By arrangement with Sony BMG Music
Entertainment

"ROCK YOU LIKE A HURRICANE"
Written by Klas Meine, Rudolf Schenker,
Herman Rarebell
Performed by Scorpions
Courtesy of The Island Def Jam Music
Group
Under license from Universal Music Enterprises

"LIGHTERS UP"
Written by K. Jones, Scott Storch, Roger
Greene Jr., Victor Carraway, Voletta Wallace
Performed by Lil' Kim
Courtesy of Atlantic Recording Corp.
By arrangement with Warner Music Group
Film & TV Licensing

"Y'ALL KNOW ME"
Written by Mike Fratantuno, Brian Lapin,
Terence Yoshiaki Graves, Josef Lord
Performed by Transcenders featuring J7
D'Star
Courtesy of Transcenders, LLC

"RONDO" from "CIRQUE DU
SOLEIL—MYSTERE"
Written by René Dupéré
Courtesy of Créations Méandres, Inc.

"REMINISCING"
Written by Graeham Goble
Performed by Little River Band
Courtesy of EMI Records
Under license from EMI Film & Television
Music

"FRUIT SALAD"
Written by Murray Cook, Jeff Fatt, Anthony
Field, Greg Page
Performed by The Wiggles
Courtesy of The Wiggles International Pty.
Ltd.

"HOT POTATO"
Written by Murray Cook, Jeff Fatt, Anthony
Field, Greg Page, John Field
Performed by The Wiggles
Courtesy of The Wiggles International Pty.
Ltd.

"HERE COME THE WIGGLES"
Written by Murray Cook, Jeff Fatt, Anthony
Field, Greg Page, Dominic Lindsay
Performed by The Wiggles
Courtesy of The Wiggles International Pty.
Ltd.

"HAPPY BIRTHDAY TO YOU"
Written by Mildred J. Hill, Patty S. Hill

"HELICOPTER" from TWO WEEKS
NOTICE
Written by John Powell
Performed by John Powell
Courtesy of Warner Bros. Entertainment

"WE ARE NOWHERE AND IT'S NOW"
Written by Conor Oberst
Performed by Bright Eyes
Courtesy of Saddle Creek

About the Writer/Director/Producer

JUDD APATOW made his feature directorial debut with the 2005 film he also produced, *The 40-Year-Old Virgin*, starring Steve Carell. He also produced *Superbad*, starring Jonah Hill, Michael Cera, Seth Rogen, and Bill Hader.

Apatow recently produced *Drillbit Taylor*, starring Owen Wilson, and the summer 2006 hit *Talladega Nights: The Ballad of Ricky Bobby*, starring Will Ferrell. He is the executive producer of the independent film *The TV Set*, a scathingly funny look at the television industry, starring David Duchovny and Sigourney Weaver. He also co-wrote *Walk Hard,* starring John C. Reilly.

He was the executive producer of *Kicking & Screaming*, starring Will Ferrell, and he produced *Anchorman: The Legend of Ron Burgundy*, starring Ferrell, Christina Applegate, and Paul Rudd.

Apatow co-wrote the screenplay for the remake of *Fun With Dick and Jane*, starring Jim Carrey and Téa Leoni. He made his feature film debut as a co-writer and executive producer on the comedy *Heavyweights*. He also served as a producer on the dark comedy *The Cable Guy*, directed by Ben Stiller and starring Jim Carrey and Matthew Broderick.

On the small screen, Apatow served as an executive producer of the award-winning series *Freaks and Geeks*, which debuted in 1999 and for which he also wrote and directed several episodes. He created and was executive producer of the series *Undeclared*, which was named one of *Time* magazine's 10 best shows of 2001.

Previously, Apatow worked as a writer, director, and producer on the series *The Larry Sanders Show*, starring Garry Shandling. For his work on the show, he earned an Emmy Award nomination for Outstanding Writing for a Comedy Series and received five consecutive Emmy Award nominations for Outstanding Comedy Series. In addition, *The Larry Sanders Show* brought Apatow five Cable ACE Awards for Best Comedy Series and a Writers Guild of America WGA Episodic Comedy Award nomination for an episode he co-wrote.

Born in Syosset, New York, Apatow aspired at an early age to become a professional comedian. While still in high school, he created a radio show and began interviewing comedy personalities he admired, including Steve Allen, Howard Stern, and John Candy. Inspired, he began performing his own stand-up routines by the end of his senior year.

Following an appearance on HBO's *Young Comedians* special, Apatow eventually stopped performing in favor of writing and went on to co-create and act as executive producer of *The Ben Stiller Show*, for which he earned an Emmy for Outstanding Individual Achievement in Writing in a Variety or Music Program.